D1003469

Make Money Blogging

9 Proven Strategies to Make Money Online

Go beyond lame blogging books with this step-by-step into nine proven systems to make money blogging

I spent years wanting to start a blog. I hated my job and knew I didn't want to spend a third of my day miserable…but looking through blogging books, all I found were generic strategies and lofty promises.

They all promised huge incomes but none really told me how much bloggers make or how to make money on a website.

I said screw it and started my blogs anyway in 2014. I quit my job and spent 60+ hours a week building my sites and learning how to make money blogging.

You know what, it paid off. I doubled my monthly income last year and now make more than 85% of bloggers. That's in just two years of blogging and I make money from seven different sources every month.

Flip-flops and a T-shirt are my uniform and I'm loving it!

You Don't Have 60+ Hours a Week to Learn about Blogging?

I didn't start making money blogging overnight. I treated it like a business, I put everything into it and sacrificed life for months to learn how to be successful.

My pain is your gain.

You don't have to sacrifice a year of your time to start making money. I put everything I learned on my own into this book from the easiest ways to make money to the methods that make thousands a month.

Making Money Blogging…and only Making Money

This isn't just another generic blogging book, covering everything from starting your blog to building traffic and then offering a side-note on a few ways to make money.

You can find that anywhere. Type 'Start a Blog' in Google and you'll find thousands of articles on how to setup your site but none of them tell you exactly how to make money. Believe me, I tried and had to learn the hard way.

This book is 100% dedicated to giving you the tools that make money on websites.

In this book you'll learn:

- The proven one-year strategy for developing different income sources on your blog, from the immediate payoffs to the methods that make thousands a month (pg. 171)

- The complete sales funnel one blogger uses to sell his $1,000 courses and make between $30,000 to $70,000 every single month (pg. 93)

- How I turned my blogs into a self-publishing engine and make nearly $2,000 a month just on the books (pg. 67)

- How I doubled the monthly income from my blogs last year to make more than 85% of bloggers (pg. 6)

- How I turned a blog making less than $100 a month into a $1,000 cash machine in less than three weeks (pg. 112)

Do you hate your job? Do you spend hours day-dreaming of early retirement?

Is it retirement you really want or just the freedom to do something you enjoy?

My Work from Home Money is your source for work at home ideas and strategies. Financial freedom isn't about having lots of money, it's about making money doing the things you enjoy…and that's exactly what this blog will help you do.

I've spent years working freelance, blogging and searching for different ways to make money. I've made more than my share of mistakes and seen more scams than I can count. I've also found countless individuals that are living their dream lives, with a successful work-at-home business.

This isn't about not working. I don't promise you a 4-Hour Work Week. What I do promise is that you'll find something you enjoy doing, that you'll find the way to make money doing it, and that you will be in control of your own financial future for the first time in your life.

Joseph Hogue, CFA

Born and raised in Iowa, I graduated from Iowa State University after serving in the Marine Corps. I worked in corporate finance and real estate before starting a career in investment analysis. I've appeared on Bloomberg as an expert in emerging market investing and led a team of equity analysts for a Canadian sell-side research firm.

Working in the corporate world, I realized there was something missing in the 9-to-5 rat race. I was making lots of money but hated my job and realized…who wants to be rich when they're old if they spent a third of their life miserable.

I now run six websites and love my work-at-home life. How much I make and my work life is completely up to me. I no longer worry about saving for retirement because I can't imagine ever doing anything else. I have published ten books on investing, passive income, crowdfunding and starting a business.

ISBN978-0-9971112-4-8 (digital)

ISBN 978-0-9971112-5-5(paperback)

Contents

How Much Money Can You Make Blogging?

Promises of six-figure incomes draw a lot of people into blogging. The idea that you can make thousands blogging from home every month sounds too good to be true.

A lot of websites and bloggers don't help. The idea of making money online has become a late-night infomercial, virtually guaranteeing success…as long as you sign up for the blogger's course.

The truth is a little different.

Just like any business, there's a lot of work that goes on behind the scenes to make a blog successful. Beyond just pecking away at the keyboard, you need to manage a range of tasks from search engine optimization to accounting and reinvesting in your business.

And you have to know how to make money!

Making money blogging, I mean making real money that turns your online properties into a business, means understanding the different ways to make money and how to use each of them strategically.

Understand this and you will not only survive the 95% failure rate on new blogs but you'll grow your blogging business every year and reach those six-figure dreams.

How Much Money do Bloggers Make?

There are two problems you'll have to face as a new blogger when it comes to making money.

First is the fact that blogs do not make much money immediately. You might only get a thousand or two visitors a month over the first six months blogging and that usually doesn't translate into much of an income.

Many of the best ways bloggers make money won't be an option over these first few months either. Sponsors aren't interested in a blog that won't get their message out to tens of thousands and you haven't built the community that will drive students to coaching or classes.

These two reasons are why most bloggers give up and stop updating their website before their six-month anniversary. More than half of bloggers in a Problogger survey reported making less than $100 a month.

How Much Do Blogs Earn?
Survey of 4,048 Bloggers

Source: Problogger.net (data)

Stick with it though and blogging can be an opportunity like no other. One-in-ten bloggers to the survey reported making more than $15,000 a month.

2

And your monthly income will grow surprisingly fast. How many jobs have you had that doubled your monthly income every year?

I just closed out my best month yet, booking nearly $5,000 last month in blogging income on top of $4,200 in freelancing income. That monthly total is more than four-times what I made in the same month last year and my goal is to double it over the next year.

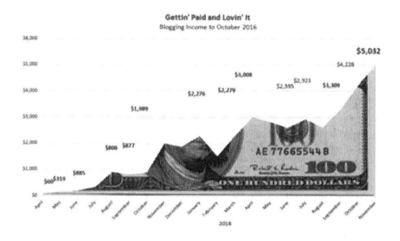

Even at that goal, I would still be just scraping the surface of what is possible with online income. I personally know bloggers that make tens of thousands a month and one that makes millions a year.

These super-successful bloggers aren't geniuses, they have no secret that helped them make money. They simply learned how to run their websites like a business and how to use different methods to make money.

How to Use this Book to Turn Your Blog into a Cash Machine

We'll cover nine of the best ways to make money blogging in the book, starting with the fastest and finishing with the ways to make big money on high-value products.

Each chapter is a step-by-step in each blogging income method, not just a quick overview, and will help you understand how much money you can expect to make.

Read through the book to get an idea of the different methods but don't feel like you must try every single one. One blogger shares how he makes between $30,000 and $70,000 each month on courses. He's got an automated process that works great and he isn't trying to fix it with other money-making ideas.

I'm a big believer in diversifying blogging income, making sure you make money on several different methods. That way, if one of those income sources dries up (and it's something that happens all the time) then you won't be left wondering how to pay the bills.

Trying different income sources also helps to see which work best for your website. I run six blogs and no two make money the same way. There's a lot of trial-and-error to it but it doesn't take long to figure out what works best for you.

When that happens, you'll make more money than you thought possible and will see it grow every year. You'll be happier than you've ever been at a traditional job. You'll have control of your financial future and will actually enjoy work!

The last chapter is a strategy for new bloggers, what to do to launch your blog and how much you can make in your first few years. Just as blogs vary in how well different income sources perform, blogger paths vary as well.

If you're starting your blog while still working a 9-to-5 then you might only be able to commit five or ten hours a week to your website. That's fine and a great way to develop your online property while still having that certainty from a full-time paycheck.

The great thing about blogging is that five or ten hours a week is all it takes to be successful and start making lots of money. The first few income sources in the book can be put together almost immediately, bringing in profits and motivating you to keep at it. After a year, you'll be ready to jump into higher-value products that earn money consistently, even if you take time off from blogging.

Before you know it, your blog will be making more than your traditional job and you'll be ready to make the transition to full-time internet entrepreneur.

I'm still amazed when people ask me if it's really possible to make money blogging, even despite everything they've heard from failed bloggers. I'm excited to share this book with you and an income strategy that will change your life just as it's changed mine.

Pay-per-Click Advertising: Your First Money-Maker

How much can you make blogging? That's usually the second question I get when I tell people I'm a blogger.

The first question is usually, "Really? That's an actual thing?"

When they find out how much I and other bloggers make running our own websites, and after picking their jaw up off the floor, they always want to know how.

This first chapter will cover making money with display advertising and ad networks on your blog.

Display advertising and ad networks isn't a particularly exciting topic and it actually doesn't make a ton of money.

Why start with it then?

Because display ads through Google Adsense and other ad networks is usually the first way most bloggers make money. It's easy and is about as passive as it gets for blogging income.

What is Display Advertising and PPC?

Display advertising is the most basic form of making money online. If you're on just about any website, look to the right sidebar or at the top of the page and you'll probably see at least one display ad.

Even the largest websites use display advertising

Online advertising is nothing more than a commercial on websites.

Yeah, I know everyone hates commercials but blogging is a business. Without blogging income from things like online advertising and affiliate ads, you wouldn't have one billion-plus websites on the 'net. Instead you'd have a few sites that basically amounted to random rants about people's day.

The way you get these ad boxes on your site is by signing up to ad networks like Google Adsense.

After signing up for an ad network, you'll be able to decide where on your blog to place ads and the types of advertising you'll allow.

The ad network will give you an html code that you can put on your site to automatically manage the online ads. We'll get to how to do this all in the rest of the chapter.

There are primarily two ways you make money on display advertising, through impressions or through clicks.

Pay-per Click Advertising (PPC) are online ads that only pay when a visitor clicks through to the advertiser. The amount you make depends on the topic, i.e. topics like insurance and lending pay much higher rates than other topics like fundraising and travel.

Never, ever click on your own PPC ads. Ad networks track where clicks come from and the visitor actions after the click. It's pretty obvious when a click is from you or someone that had no intention of buying the product. Trying to cheat the ad networks will get you banned fast.

Pay-per Mille Advertising (PPM) will look the same as PPC but you get paid based on the number of times the ad shows on your site, the impressions. Mille is latin for thousand, which is the basic unit in which PPM ads are measured. You will make a set amount, usually from $2 to $12, for every thousand times the display ad is shown.

Most Google Adsense advertising is the PPC variety while other ad networks use a combination of both. I've found that both work out to be pretty close to the same amount of money.

I've seen about 0.004% of impressions result in a click by a visitor and averaged $1.30 per click. That works out to about $5.20 per mille which is the standard rate for starter rates on Google Adsense and some networks.

Build your site large enough to get on more exclusive networks and you can get rates as high as $12 per mille, which can be thousands a month even on this basic money-making method.

The ad network does a lot of technical stuff in the background that really isn't important. Most ad networks will use cookies to track a web user's activity and then publish the most relevant ads on your blog.

That's an important point in case you missed it. The ads you see on your blog won't necessarily be the same other visitors see. It depends on what other sites they visit and products they view along with the content on your blog. That's a good thing because it makes the ad more relevant and more likely the visitor will click on it.

Ad Network Vocabulary

Impression – The number of times a visitor sees one of your ads. This will be different from your page views because you might have multiple display ads on one page. Ads placed higher up on the page will get more impressions than those further down.

Cost per Click (CPC) – the amount an advertiser pays the ad network for display advertising. The ad network will take its profit and then put the rest in your account. CPC will vary by topic and country.

Cost per Mille (CPM) – the amount an advertiser pays the ad network for PPM ads. Beyond the way these ads are paid, by impression and not by the click, everything else is the same as pay-per-click advertising.

Click through Rate (CTR) – the percentage of clicks per every 100 times an ad is shown. For example, if eight people click on an ad for every 1,000 impressions then you have a 0.8% CTR.

Ad Zone – This is the location on your blog where ads are shown. Common ad zones are in the header, sidebar and various places in each post.

Fill Rate – The percentage of actual display ads shown relative to the total number of potential impressions. If you have three ad zones on a page and it gets 50,000 page views then you have a potential of 150,000 impressions on that page. Because ad networks aren't always able to find an appropriate ad, you won't usually have all those potential impressions filled.

Think of it as the ad network didn't have enough commercials appropriate to your site to show. If the page ends up only showing 120,000 impressions, then you have an 80% fill rate.

Pros and Cons of Display Advertising for Bloggers

- Easy to use. There is really no effort beyond the initial setup for display advertising.

- Faster to pay out than other blog income streams. You can get on some ad networks almost immediately after starting a blog.

- Lower payout compared to other blogging income streams. Maybe it's not an entirely fair comparison since I don't use online advertising as much as affiliates but I make about 15-times more on affiliate income as I do display ads.

- Too many ads can be intrusive and a poor visitor experience.

- Less control of what appears on your blog. There are ways to control the topics advertised on your blog but there will always be some that squeeze through the cracks.

How Much Money Can You Make with Online Advertising?

The ease of making money through online advertising is balanced by the fact that it won't account for a big portion of your blogging income. Below is a graphic of my display ad income over the 16 months through August 2016.

Making Money with Online Advertising
PPC and Ad Network Revenue for Bloggers

Source: My Work from Home Money   2016

Don't give up on display ads just yet. It's not much but understand that I've never used PPC advertising as a focus to making money on my blogs. By the time I started putting ads on the sites, I was already making money on self-publishing, consulting and freelancing.

Filling ad space with my own products and services was worth more than loading up the blog with display ads. I started with just a few Google ads and started taking most of those down this year to promote affiliates and other income streams.

That said, I still make between $0.005 and $0.013 per page view over the period with online advertising.

I've seen older blogs that focus on display ads make much more on a monthly basis. One blogger I know makes over $2,000 each month through ad networks and Google Adsense. She averages over 300.000 page views a month and makes much more on other income streams but it still proves that you can make money on ads as well.

Would you turn down an extra $2,000 a month?

The amount you can make on display ads is actually secondary to the motivation it can provide. The vast majority of bloggers quit within six months of launching their site for lack of making any money. Even making $100 a month on your new blog can be enough to keep you going to eventually start making thousands.

There is another option beyond ad networks through direct advertising. This is where you contract with companies directly to show their display ad and get paid either on a pay-per-click or a per impression basis.

We'll focus on ad networks at the expense of covering direct advertising because…well not that many bloggers use direct advertising. The ad networks have made a very good business out of making online advertising profitable for bloggers. New bloggers with limited traffic aren't going to get much on direct ads and bloggers with larger sites can get on some of the more exclusive ad networks that pay better rates.

Getting Started with Google Adsense

Google Adsense is the ad network most bloggers start on because of its lower eligibility requirements. To start showing ads through the network, you only need to be 18 years old, have a hosted blog and have legitimate content on the site. I've heard rumors that your blog needs to be at least four to six months old but have also talked to bloggers that were approved much earlier.

Google makes money…a ton of money by showing online ads in its search as well as on websites through its Adsense program. The company made $16.4 billion last year on its 'network' advertising which means bloggers and websites made just over $17 billion.

While other ad networks may pay higher rates, they can be more difficult to get on and can't usually fill as much of your ad space as Google. Google works with so many more advertisers that it can almost always fill your ad zones completely.

That translates to more money blogging even if rates are a little lower compared to other ad networks.

Getting started on Google Adsense is extremely easy with just a few screens of basic information.

There are very few areas that will trip you up in getting started.

- Your 'payee name' on your payment information should be the same as that on your bank account.

- Google restricts some of the email providers you can use to sign up but will accept the larger ones like Gmail, Hotmail and most hosted email accounts attached to your website.

Signing up and filling out your information takes less than half an hour including the tax information you need to get paid.

I recommend installing the Google Adsense plugin on your website. It makes it super easy to configure your account and place ads on your blog. Normally, you would need to copy code from the Adsense platform to the places on your blog where you want ads to run. With the plugin, you simply select the parts of your page for ads.

You will have different layouts for your home page, blog page, categories and other pages.

Once you're all set up, Google will continuously analyze your site and each visitor for the best display ads to show. Google uses a bidding competition in its decision to place advertising so you can be sure that the highest paying ad that is appropriate to your content and a visitor's interests is shown.

While most of the work is done for you, there is one thing you will want to check in the Google Adsense platform.

Click on 'Allow & Block Ads' in the top menu and then the 'Sensitive Categories' tab.

You can choose to disallow ads in these categories, from specific advertisers and from more general categories. Besides these sensitive categories, some bloggers choose to block ads that would be in direct competition with their own products and services.

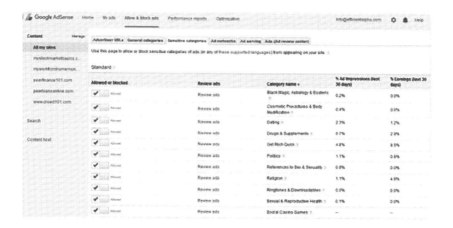

You can log into your Adsense account at any time and see real-time earnings but you will only get paid once your total earnings are above a threshold amount.

We'll go over a more detailed advertising strategy later in the post but some basic ideas to keep in mind when using Google Adsense:

- You are allowed to place up to three display ads and two text units on each page. Display ads are images while the text units are lines of clickable text.

- I don't do any advertising on my home page. You want your home page to be your brand message, not a place that takes visitors away from the blog through advertising.

- Ads within your articles can be effective but there can be a conflict with images in the post, leading to large chunks of white space if an image and ad zone end up on top of each other.

- Ads in the sidebar, that right margin area, usually aren't as effective but get lots of impressions. Balance ad space with links to other articles, ads for your own products and your email callout.

Making More Money with Ad Networks

So we've already walked through one ad network, Google Adsense. I've talked with bloggers that only ever use Google for their display ads and are perfectly happy with it. Google has so many advertisers in its network that it can fill almost 100% of your ad space.

The problem with Google is that it takes a big cut of the profits (49%) and the price it's been charging advertisers has been going down for years.

If you really want to make money with online advertising, you need to use multiple ad networks. We'll list out a few good ones here and a strategy for maximizing how much money you make later in the article.

Instant Approval Ad Networks

If you've just started blogging or don't meet some of Google's requirements for Adsense (though they're pretty easy), there are a few ad networks that let just about anyone serve ads. These networks won't pay as much for ads but it's a good place to start and can still be a good complement to your Adsense earnings.

Chitika used to be one of the largest and most popular ad networks but has fallen behind against Google and some of the premium display networks. It's still a strong contender and has the advantage of no traffic minimum.

Chitika ads are responsive and customer service is among the best I've seen in online advertising networks. The minimum payout is just $10 so even smaller blogs with very low traffic can see a check within a month or two.

PopAds also has no minimum traffic requirements and accepts nearly any blog into its ad network, including 'adult' websites. The CPM rates tend to be a little higher compared to other instant approval ad networks and the minimum payout ($5) is the lowest I've seen.

PopAds is interesting because it serves pop-under ads, those boxes that open a new internet browser for a display ad, as well as the traditional on-site display ads. It's very popular with the adult sites since they can't get approved for Google Ads but can also be an option for other blogs as well. CPM rates tend to be around $2.50 per thousand impressions.

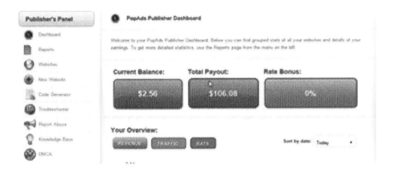

Revenue Hits pays out much like affiliates so you won't get paid just for impressions or clicks. The ad placement works automatically like display advertising but the platform will track clicks through to purchases.

I have seen rates from $10 up to $50 which isn't great for affiliate advertising but is still ok for display advertising. The network offers instant activation so that's a plus but I would check out some of the other ad networks first.

Premium Ad Networks

While the BlogHer ad network doesn't require a minimum traffic number, they are pickier about approvals than the instant approval networks above. You need to be updating your blog at least once or twice a week and generally need a female-focus for your audience.

If you get accepted to the network, you'll need to show at least one ad above-the-fold and may not get paid for some of the public service announcements the network pushes through to blogs.

AdThrive is one of the most popular premium ad networks and great for blogs a few years old. There are two programs, one for blogs with at least 75,000 monthly visitors and another for blogs with at least 100k visitors. AdThrive is a full-service ad network and basically takes over your ad space to optimize your blog income. Clients report an average increase of 249% over their previous ad network income.

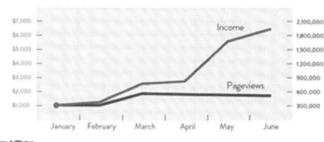

Actual Client Income Results

This blogger's traffic increased 70% over a six-month period, but her overall earnings increased 700%.

Source: AdThrive

Adsterra requires publishers to have a minimum of 300,000 visitors per month but offers a lot of formats including pushups, pop-unders, sliders, display ads and interstitials to serve lots of ads on your site. Ads are also offered on a CPM, CPC and cost-per-action basis.

**Complete Display Advertising Strategy for
PPC and Ad Networks**

Getting set up with ad networks and putting display ads on your blog is the easy part. You'll make money with ads on your site but can make a lot more by optimizing your display advertising strategy.

That means using the best ad sizes, formats and making sure you fill as much of your ad space as possible.

Best Banner Sizes and Display Ad Placement

While you'll want to try out different display ad image sizes and the best place to put them on your site, there are some tips you can use to get started.

The best places to put ads are where people look…shock! Check out the online advertising placement graphic below. It shows research results of where bloggers tend to get the highest click through rate on advertising.

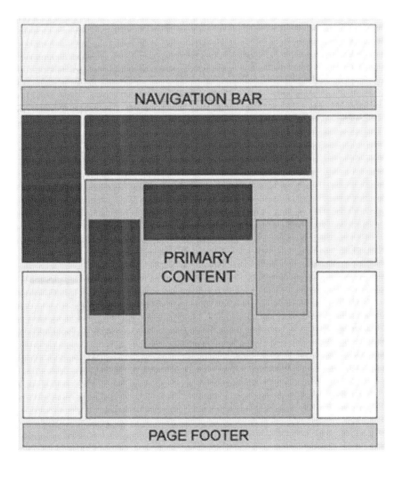

Red areas are the best, followed by cream and then yellow.

Years of display advertising in the right sidebar has made it a pretty lame place to put ads. Readers ignore this area almost on a sub-conscious level. I usually have one ad zone in the sidebar but save the rest to highlight most popular articles, reviews and social sharing.

The upside to the sidebar and the header, which performs relatively well, is that you get a ton of impressions. Think about it, any ad you have in the header is going to show on every single page. Even at a low CTR, it will still mean clicks on a higher number of impressions.

One of the reasons I've moved away from display advertising is that the best performing places to put your ads are also the most intrusive to your readers. I hate reading a blog post and having to scroll through a banner add ever few paragraphs.

Some bloggers have even switched to a left-hand sidebar. Since readers aren't used to the left-sidebar and because English-speakers read left to right, the alternate positioning gets more attention. Personally, I think it's a little annoying because your eye naturally goes clear to the left side into the side bar while reading.

It shouldn't come as a surprise that the best performing display ad banner sizes are the larger ones. In fact, the half page banner size had a CTR of more than seven-times that of the 468x60 banner in a test by Digital Inspiration.

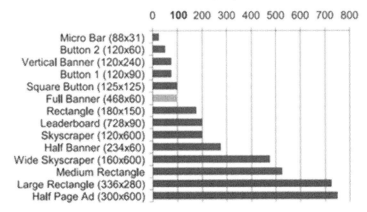

The numbers are the pixel size of the ad image, first the horizontal then the vertical.

The medium rectangle size in the graphic is the 300x250 pixel banner size. I've found the relatively square banner sizes (300x250 and 336x280) work really well in a sidebar while the leader board is the most commonly used in headers.

Banners versus Text Ads to Make More Money

Banner ads suck. There, I said it.

When I started blogging, I just assumed that big image ads would make money. How can your eye not be attracted to a big picture on the page?

The problem is that web users have gotten so accustom to seeing online advertising that they almost completely ignore banner display ads. It's too obvious that these ads are commercials. Visitors are naturally skeptical from the start and click through rates are notoriously low for banner ads, around 0.2% and even lower.

Use text ads instead when you can.

Which brings us to…Link Ads

Make More Money with Link Ads

One effective but often overlooked ad is the text link ad. This is a few lines of clickable text rather than a large display ad. There are a couple of reasons why I like link ads and why they should be part of your online advertising strategy.

- You are only allowed up to three display ads on each page for Google Adsense but can add another two link ads

- Link ads are less intrusive than banner ads. They take up less space and blend in with the rest of the content on your page.

- Link ads get a better click through rate than banner ads. The text ads look less like a commercial and more like a resource to readers.

To set up your link ads, follow the steps below.

1. Click on 'My Ads' and then 'New Ad Unit' on the Google Adsense platform. You can name the ad anything you want.

2. Change the Ad Size to Link Ads by clicking on the box next to 'Showing' and leave 'Responsive Links' highlighted.

3. You can change the ad style and custom channels if you like but go with the defaults to start.

4. Click on 'Save and Get Code'

Click save and a popup box will appear with your ad unit code. You then log in to WordPress, go to 'Appearance' and 'Widgets'. It is here where you can put the code in a text box anywhere you like. This is also the process you would use for other display ads if you were not using the Adsense plugin or if you want to customize some of your ad placements.

I like to add link ads to just under the main menu on the blog page and under a list of 'Most Popular' posts. The idea is that the link ads blend in with these sections and visitors are more likely to click on the ad.

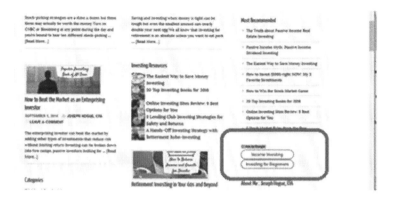

Maximizing your Ad Network Income with a Waterfall Strategy

Because of the limited list of advertisers on most ad networks, you may not get all your ad zones filled on your blog if you use just one network. Think about it, the ad network only has so many advertisers that are appropriate to your blog and audience. If you are large enough to get accepted on some ad networks, you could have impressions well into the hundreds of thousands.

Remember the term 'Fill Rate'? It's the percentage of your total available ad space that is actually filled. Most ad networks besides Google Adsense have fill rates between 20% and 40% and even lower during times of the year where ad buying drops off.

This is why creating a waterfall strategy, also called a daisy chain, is so important.

A waterfall is instructions you give your ad network to determine who fills your ad zones. It's a fairly easy process:

1. Put the ad network code on your blog to begin serving display ads

2. Go to your ad network platform

3. Set up a backfill, ask customer service if you cannot find where to do this

4. You will enter the Google Adsense code for each ad zone as a backfill

5. The idea is to have the premium ad network first try to fill the ad placement, if they can't place an ad then Google Adsense does it

Google has so many advertisers that it boasts a 100% fill rate so this strategy will fill your maximum ad potential. You may even try placing another ad network in-between so that you have two premium networks trying to fill ads before Google takes over. Understand that each spot will mean a delay in an ad being placed so you don't want to have more than two ad networks in your waterfall before sending the request to Google.

The waterfall strategy will maximize both your fill rate, making sure you always have an ad show where you want it, and the amount of income you get from those ads. Google ads don't usually pay as much as the premium networks and the search engine behemoth takes a bigger slice of the pie. Filling your display ads with premium networks when available means more money while still filling with Google if necessary.

Ad networks and display advertising may become a smaller part of your blogging income as you grow your online asset but it could be one of the best income streams for new bloggers. Online advertising is growing every year and you can get instant approval on some ad networks to start making money immediately.

Affiliate Income:
Where the Big Money Starts

Affiliate marketing has saved my butt more than a few times with my blogging income. It was one of the first revenue streams I implemented and the first to make serious money.

We'll cover everything affiliate here including my process for affiliate marketing, how much you can make and how to do affiliate marketing without seeming spammy.

What is Affiliate Marketing

Affiliate marketing is a form of advertising on your blog. You place a link or a banner to a product on the site or in an article. If someone clicks through the advertisement and buys the product, you receive a commission.

That's different from how you make money with other types of advertising like with Google Adsense. In Pay-per-Click (PPC) ads, you only need someone to click on a link or banner to get paid.

With affiliate marketing, you might have hundreds of people click on the link before anyone actually buys the product and you might need hundreds of people to see the link for every five or ten clicks.

The upside is that affiliate marketing pays much more for each commission. You'll get anywhere from a couple of bucks to hundreds when you make an affiliate sale.

Advertisers like affiliate sales because they only pay when someone buys their product. It can save a lot of money versus throwing funds at Google Adwords and the PPC model.

Bloggers like affiliate marketing because it can lead to a lot more money if they promote the right affiliates. You also don't have to create your own products to start making money. When someone clicks on your link, a code (cookie) is placed on their computer. The cookie can last from a few days to months, depending on the advertiser, and you get credit for any purchases made during that time.

We'll go into the complete How-To process of how to start making money below. The easiest way is to join affiliate networks, middleman websites that work with advertisers. You create an account and can apply to advertise hundreds of affiliates. You get all your links from the one place and get all your commissions in one check.

1) Join an Affiliate Network
2) Add your Blogs
3) Apply to Advertisers
4) Get your Affiliate Links
5) Copy Links into a Post or Page
6) Get Paid!!

How Much Can You Make with Affiliates?

I make just under two grand on affiliates each month, about a third of the income from the blogs. That's really only on two of my blogs since the other four blogs are still fairly new and I'm still building traffic to the point where affiliate sales are higher.

Affiliate sales are usually higher in some months versus others. This is called seasonality and it's a factor in affiliate marketing. It will be different for some affiliates but most see higher sales before and during the holidays while activity trails off during the spring and summer.

That's a problem in a lot of blogging income streams. People are less inclined to buy stuff, take courses, ask for consulting or do just about anything during the summer. There are two ways to approach it:

- Don't worry about it. The money you make on affiliate marketing will grow each year as your blog grows. Some months will be lower but the trend will be upwards. Enjoy the good months and put a little extra in savings.

- Diversify by signing up for affiliate programs that do well in spring and summer months (i.e. gift ideas around Mothers' and Fathers' Day, summer travel, etc.). Advertising has to be natural to your topic but the more affiliates you talk about, the more likely you are to build a consistent income stream.

I've balanced my affiliate sales with other income streams so not all my posts are monetized through an affiliate link. If you focus more directly on affiliates, you can make a lot more each month.

Rakuten Marketing released a survey earlier this year with publishers reporting making more than 20% of their total website income from affiliates.

I know bloggers that make tens of thousands a month on affiliate sales…yes, that's $10,000+ in a single month. There's no secret to it. Just a simple process outlined below and the website traffic to get clicks.

It's not just how much you can make with affiliate marketing but the ease at which you do it. While some of the other blogging income streams require hours spent on writing, course creation or other services, affiliate marketing takes almost no time to put links in your articles. Even better, there is almost no upkeep – you'll continue to make passive income from affiliate links on old posts.

The same Rakuten survey projects affiliate marketing sales to grow at an annual rate of 10% through 2020 to $6.8 billion. That's just over the expected growth rate for all online sales and way over the 4% growth expected in traditional store retail sales.

If you have a blog…you need to be taking advantage of affiliate marketing as an income stream!

Joining Affiliate Networks for Blogging Income

There are a few different ways to promote affiliate marketing on your blog. The most common is by joining affiliate networks to find advertisers.

These affiliate networks seek out and negotiate with advertisers on their programs. You create an account on the network and search for advertisers within different categories.

You usually need to apply for each advertiser's affiliate program so it's a good idea to search through and apply for all the ones you might be interested in joining before you need the links.

Each advertiser on the network will have rules to their program, where you may use the links and what is prohibited. These are generally the same for most advertisers and include things like not bidding on Google Adsense keywords around the advertiser's branded name. Some advertisers will let you place their links on social media sites or in emails.

Keep the rules and details for all your affiliates on a spreadsheet so you remember which allow different kinds of sharing. Breaking the rules can void sales or get you kicked off an affiliate program.

Each advertiser will also disclose how much money you make on each sale, either a commission rate or a flat fee. Also disclosed will be the cookie duration, the amount of time during which you will get credit for a sale made by someone that clicks through your link. I've seen these as low as a few days and as long as 60-days.

Along with your account, you will input your payment information. Most affiliate networks offer electronic deposits into your checking account. You will generally be paid on a monthly basis, usually for the previous month sales.

Some affiliate networks to check out:

ShareaSale – One of the longest-running and largest affiliate networks with more than 16 years in affiliate marketing

CJ Affiliates – Formerly Commission Junction and my top affiliate network

Flexoffers – A bit smaller than the other networks and with limited reporting but still worth the time

LinkShare (Rakuten) – Bills itself as the #1 affiliate marketing network…though I'm not sure how they measure it. Lots of advertisers and an easy dashboard.

You can join more than one affiliate network. In fact, I have an account on all four networks above. It doesn't cost anything to join and being on more than one network gives you a greater range of advertisers to promote.

If you run multiple blogs, you will need to add each to your affiliate network accounts. When you go to copy the links for an advertiser to promote on a blog, you will need to make sure you are using the link approved for the specific blog. We'll cover this more in detail later.

Joining Amazon Associates Affiliate Program

Amazon has its own affiliate program that you will also want to join called Amazon Associates. You can create one account for all your blogs and do not have to use separate links for the same product when posting on different websites.

Amazon makes it extremely easy to get links and promote products on your blog. These easiest way is directly from the website but you can also use the Amazon Associates site to search for links.

The downside to Amazon Associates affiliate marketing is the terms and payout on sales. You only get credit for a purchase if a reader buys something within one day of clicking on your link. If they add the product to their shopping cart then you get credit if they buy the item within 90-days but otherwise, it's the shortest cookie duration I've seen anywhere.

TABLE 1 – Fixed Advertising Fee Rates for Specific Product Categories

Product Category	Fixed Advertising Fee Rates
Electronics Products (including all Office Products)	4.00%
Television Products	2.00%
PC Component Products	2.50%
Kindle tablets, Kindle e-readers, and Fire Phone	4.00%
Amazon Fire TV and Echo	7.00%
Amazon MP3 Products	5.00%
Amazon Video Products	5.00%
Game Downloads Products	10.00%
Gift Cards Redeemable on amazon.com	6.00%
Gift Cards Not Redeemable on amazon.com	4.00%
Amazon Coins	10.00%
Grocery Products (including Prime Pantry)	4.00%
Video Game Console Products	1.00%
Headphones Products	6.00%
DVD Products	4.00%
Industrial Products	8.00%

Source: Amazon Associates

The other downside is the payout, ranging from just 2% of sales on televisions to 10% on game downloads and coins. Even the 10% rate is pitifully low compared to most affiliate marketing advertisers that offer commissions as high as 70% on their products.

For products not listed in the chart, your commission starts at 4% and is adjusted higher depending on the number of items shipped in any given month. These rates suck but you can still make money with Amazon affiliate marketing.

You will earn a commission when someone clicks on your Amazon Associates link but then buys something else on the site. Most of your readers are going to be fairly comfortable buying on Amazon so you do not have to get over that 'brand awareness' hurdle that you might with other affiliate advertisers.

I've found reviews and list comparisons work well for selling Amazon products. One example is a 'best books' list I run each year for each blog.

1. Pick a fairly narrow keyword like 'best investing books' for which you think you can rank on Google. This is important because it will send you consistent traffic each month to the post.

2. Look for ten or more products within the topic, i.e. books you have read or popular books within the theme.

3. Provide a one or two paragraph description of the product, who should use it and how it stacks up against the group of products. Include an image of the product in your post and tag both the name of the product in the description and the image with your affiliate link.

I've used this idea for book lists, comparing electronics in a theme and in a cord-cutting article. It isn't a big chunk of blogging income each month, around $70 currently, but it is passive income and articles generate clicks for years after they are written.

Direct Affiliates on Products You Use

Some companies don't work through affiliate networks but run their own program through their website. It's more common with individuals selling their own course or product but I've seen larger companies manage their own program as well.

The process to sign up and make money on direct affiliates is the same as working through a network. The only difference is that you only have the one product to promote from that account.

If you use a product and would like to promote it, search Google for '[company name] affiliate program' or look on the company's website at the bottom of the page.

I have done direct affiliates with a few other bloggers and their courses but don't promote direct affiliates as much as I do those on the affiliate networks. You generally don't get as much reporting with direct affiliates so you may not know how many impressions or clicks you get from the links. Working with the individual companies for just one affiliate product is a pain as well compared to the larger networks.

If the product or course is something you really love and think your readers will too, go ahead and sign up for the affiliate program. Otherwise, I would stick with the affiliate networks and Amazon. They have more products than you'll ever be able to promote and make it convenient to get all your links in one place.

How to Make Money Blogging with Affiliates

So we're finally through the introductory material on making money with affiliate marketing. Yay! Now we can get to the actual process I've used to make almost $2k a month with blog affiliates.

Some points to keep in mind before you get started with affiliate marketing on your blogs:

- **Don't burn your readers with bad products.** Wonder why affiliates offer such juicy commissions on each sale? Because it's tough (and expensive) to get new customers. The same thing goes for blog followers. Make a habit of pushing shoddy products just because they offer an affiliate payout and you'll see your blog traffic suffer.

- **Stay close to your blog topic for affiliate products.** Most blogs attract a specific type of visitor, someone looking for a specific topic whether its investing advice, personal finance tips or how to cook a soufflé. Pushing a bunch of unrelated products, i.e. the hot new smartphone on your cooking blog, isn't going to be effective. There are plenty of affiliate products available in any niche. Spend your time reviewing and talking about those and you'll make more money in less time.

- **Focus on Trust and Relationships.** Success with affiliate marketing is all about trust. If your readers feel they know you and can trust your recommendations, you'll make boatloads of money. If you write in an impersonal, sales-y way to push products…you'll just be ignored like any other commercial.

- **Create a Resource Page.** You should have a page on your site, highlighted in the menu, that shares all your best recommendations. Write up a paragraph for each affiliate and link any related articles or reviews as well as posting your affiliate link.

- **Banner Ads Suck!** Readers just don't click on banner ads that much. I use them sparingly in the sidebar on my blogs but not much elsewhere. A text link is much more effective and seems less intrusive to readers.

Once you've created your account on an ad network, you need to add your domains and payment information. You'll need an address, SSN or business EIN, checking account number and the routing number for your bank to set up electronic payments.

For each blog on which you want to place links; you'll need to fill in the domain address, some information on visitors, blog niche and a short description about the site.

Once you've got your account set up and domains added, you can start applying for affiliate programs. Just to clarify...one affiliate network contracts with thousands of companies wanting to sell their products. Each company offers publishers (bloggers) a commission and terms on their program. As a blogger, it's your job to search through the affiliates on the blog network to find the best to work with and promote.

So the question becomes...which affiliate products should I promote on my blog?

We've already hit on relevancy for your blog. You aren't going to make many affiliate sales for sports equipment on your investing blog. Writing reviews about or promoting products unrelated to your blog topic will annoy visitors and confuse Google when it comes to ranking your site.

Here's four more ways to find affiliate programs to promote on your blog.

- Products or services you already use. Think through the processes you talk about in some of your blog posts. If it's a cooking blog, what cookware do you use? What equipment or appliances do you use? Promoting products that you already use is going to go a long way to make affiliate sales based on that idea of trust.

- Check out other blogs in your niche. Most blogs will have a resource page and reviews (search for 'review' if you can't find them). Look at the links on these pages. If the link looks like a jumbled mess then it's an affiliate link. If the link is the website URL plus the name of the product then it's probably also an affiliate. You could always click through the link as well. If it goes straight to the product's sales page, it's an affiliate.

- Check out other blogger's income reports if they post them. Some will talk about their best affiliates and even detail how much they made during the month.
    - The affiliate networks listed above all have easy category search systems. Scroll through some of the categories that look applicable to your blog niche. When deciding whether to apply for an affiliate program, I look at two things: What is the affiliates three-month earnings per hundred clicks

(EPC)? This is the average earnings other bloggers have booked.

- o How long is the cookie duration? I like to see at least a 30-day cookie duration on an affiliate program. That means someone can click on my link, look over the offer but then has up to 30-days to make a purchase and I'll still get credit. If a reader has to make a buy decision immediately for me to get credit…I'll probably pass.

Click 'Apply' and agree to the terms of service on the affiliate programs you want to join. Don't feel like you have to join hundreds of programs. I've collected sales on 26 affiliate programs but just seven of them account for 90% of my total affiliate income.

There's an important message there so let's repeat it. A handful of affiliates will probably account for the vast majority of your sales. They are going to be a few affiliates that are really helpful to your blog's core market. Find out who that market is and what they need and you'll strike affiliate gold!

These best affiliate programs are probably going to be the products and services which you use and trust the most. You'll be most enthusiastic and informed about these products and readers will pick up on that.

One of my best performing affiliates is Motif Investing, an investing platform that lets you group up to 30 stocks and then buy them all with one commission. As an investor and investment analyst of more than a decade, I've never seen anything like it and I've moved much of my own money to the platform. That's a huge vote of confidence in the service and a lot of readers have followed me to the site.

Putting Affiliate Marketing Links on Your Blog

It will take up to a week for your applications to affiliate programs to be approved. This is why you should apply early and not the day before you want to post a great affiliate review on your blog.

Once approved, you'll be able to go into the affiliate network and get links or banners to put on your blog. This html code will redirect visitors to the affiliate program's website when it's clicked but also has a special part that make sure the company knows that customer came from your blog.

Most affiliate programs will have many text links and banners from which to choose. The text links will display the product or company name or up to a sentence of text that will be underlined and linked on your blog. Banner ads will also be html code but will show up as a clickable image on your site.

Some affiliate networks allow you to sort links by the highest earnings over a period. This is helpful in seeing which have converted best either because of persuasive text or a strong landing page where the link redirects. Click through the link to see where it redirects and if you think it would convert well with your readers.

When you've found a link you like, you can copy/paste the code onto a document with all your affiliate codes for reference. You are going to be promoting the affiliate often and on different posts so having a document with all your codes makes it easier than going back to the affiliate network for every post.

Again, I run very few banner ads on my sites because they just don't convert very well to sales. Your experience may be different so do some testing over a few months.

- Best places to try banner ads will be in your header, in the upper-right next to your logo, and within your sidebar. Generally the best banner sizes that fit here and convert well are the 728x90 rectangle for the header and the 300x600 or 336x280 rectangle ads in your sidebar. I will also use the slightly smaller 300x250 box-size in the side bar just to save space for content links.

- The affiliate networks will show you from which links you are getting clicks and sales so you will be able to see which banners are converting best.

- You can also place banner affiliate ads on pages or within individual posts. These convert best when they are around content related to the product, otherwise it's just a random commercial.

Affiliate links should appear natural in your blog posts or pages. This means making it look less like a commercial and more like a recommendation.

- Writing your article, link the first or second reference of the product company with your affiliate code. Either use one of the affiliate text links with the company/product name or the PrettyLink software I talk about below.

- I usually include one or two callouts as well. These are short, one-sentence calls to action that are linked. Something like, "Click here for…" or "Get this special offer from…" You'll find some of the best callouts are provided as text links on the affiliate network platform.

- You want one callout fairly soon in the article and one within the last few paragraphs. This catches the people that don't read the whole posts and those that stick around for all the info.

- Using your affiliate link code in WordPress is easy. Click the 'Text' tab in the upper-right corner of your content manager to see the html version of your post. Paste your affiliate code where you want it to appear in the article.

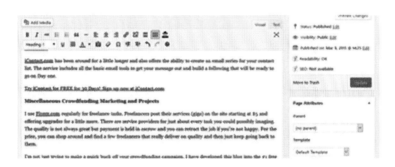

The Federal Trade Commission (FTC) requires advertisers to notify readers about paid arrangements like affiliate advertising. This is usually with a simple sentence like, "This post contains affiliate links," somewhere on the page. Some advertisers and affiliate networks are starting to require the disclosure at the top of the page in plain sight rather than hidden elsewhere.

The Best Affiliate Marketing Plugin to Make Life Simpler

Two huge pains in the neck for bloggers is managing all the link codes for affiliate programs and managing the links on their websites.

- You might have many link codes for each affiliate depending on what you want the text content to say. Going to the affiliate network dashboard or even to your link codes document every time you write a post is a nuisance. Over years of blogging, you might refer to a specific affiliate product hundreds of times in posts, reviews and pages. That is a lot of individual links to manage.

- Affiliate programs are constantly being paused, deactivated and then reactivated. You'll get emails from the affiliate network that a program has lapsed. You rush in to change the affiliate links in your posts because those programs are no longer paying...and then you get an email that the program has been reactivated. It happens a lot.

One plugin helps you manage both of these problems and it's extremely popular among bloggers. In fact, anytime you see a product mention on a site and the link URL looks like http://[blogger's website URL]/[product name] – it's probably this plugin working.

The plugin is called Pretty Links. It offers a few other features but the real power is in managing your affiliate links. By pasting in your affiliate link code in the 'Target URL' and then typing the affiliate program name or product in the 'Pretty Link' box, you create a single link you can use for every time you refer to an affiliate.

Whenever you want to link to an affiliate in a post, you just link to that new 'Pretty Link' instead of using your link code. You can link any text you want including the product name or a callout sentence.

As the name implies, the plugin also lets you change the URL link from a jumbled, messy affiliate code to something that looks more professional. Readers are hesitant about clicking on a link if they think it will take them to…

http://www.jdoqocy.com/click-7903277-11204587-1455624628000

,but will click on a link that looks like it redirects to a page on your website.

If the links for an affiliate program are ever changed or the program is deactivated on the affiliate network, all you have to do is go back and change the 'Target URL' box to redirect all the instances of that link to a new website.

The Pretty Link plugin also lets you automatically NoFollow links so you don't get in trouble with Google. The plugin tracks how many clicks you get on a link and you can download a spreadsheet showing when you got the clicks and from posts to really track your affiliate efforts.

The Pretty Link plugin comes in two prices, one allowing you to use on one website and another allowing you to use on unlimited websites. Both plans offer special training material, lifetime automatic updates and premium support.

I use the Developer Edition ($97) since I need to use it on my six websites. The Blogger Edition is cheaper ($47) but you're limited if you ever want to use it on another site.

9 Affiliate Marketing Blogging Strategies

Here are some of my favorite affiliate marketing strategies to use on a blog, in order of effectiveness. You will need to check the affiliate permissions for some of them. Some affiliate advertisers do not allow sharing their links directly on social media, though linking to an article that includes an affiliate link is always allowed.

Others prohibit email advertising or search advertising. This is why it's important to keep a spreadsheet of your affiliates along with any special rules so you don't have to continuously login to the affiliate network.

1) If you have already been blogging but haven't yet used affiliate links in your posts, the first thing you'll want to do is perform a **site audit for affiliate opportunities**. It's much easier to monetize a post that is already getting good traffic than to write a new post and hope it gets traffic.

- Go to Google Analytics then to Behavior – Site Content – All Pages in the left-hand menu. This will give you a list of the most popular posts or pages on your blog over the last month or whatever time period you set.

- Work your way down the list, looking for any natural product mentions you can make in each post. You'll want to do this with all the posts on your blog but starting with these most popular articles will get you making money faster.

- Don't force an affiliate product into a post but there is usually at least one product or service you can recommend in every post. If you're having trouble, go back to search the categories on the affiliate networks.

- Add at least a paragraph leading in to the recommendation along with your affiliate link and update the posts. The higher up you can add the link on the page, the more people will see it and the more money you'll make.

2) **My best performing affiliate posts are long comparison guides**. These are super-long articles listing out different products or services for a specific need, i.e. Best Online Loan Platforms for Bad Credit. Set up the article with a brief introduction and then launch into two or three paragraphs on each product. Include an image of each as well as special features and promotions.

These comparison posts work great for a couple of reasons. First, the length and detail generally do very well on Google. One of my comparison posts is nearly 4,000 words long and the most popular article on the blog because of all the Google traffic it gets. These posts also work because they give readers a choice. It's less about an individual product and more about helping the reader find a solution to their need.

3) **Individual reviews of affiliate products** tend to also do well. These are an entire article focusing on one product and the need it solves. Be honest and share what you didn't like about the

product as well. Talk about who specifically the product is best for and who might find a better option in another choice. Is it the low-cost option or better for one particular type of customer?

Individual reviews tend to do well because they can rank better on Google. You might have a hard time ranking a comparison post around a general keyword but add in the product name and you narrow search competition down significantly. You also get people that are looking at that specific product and might be further along in the buying decision.

It's important here to talk about buyer intent and mood and how it relates to affiliate success. When you're writing a review or comparison, try optimizing for keywords that attract search visitors close to the final purchase decision.

Before someone makes a purchase, they go through a decision process. First they have to realize they need something, even if it's on a subconscious-level. Then they look for information about products or services before evaluating the alternatives. This process may happen very quickly for impulse purchases or slowly and methodically for other purchases.

The idea is to optimize your affiliate articles for keywords around the last stages of buyer decision, when someone has the intent to buy and just needs to make a choice on a specific product.

Good Buyer Intent Keywords

Affiliate articles optimized around these words plus a product category or specific affiliate will get search traffic from people ready to make a purchase.

Review	Buy	Offer
Pros & Cons	Get	Best
FAQ	Bargain	Code
Discount	Coupon	Step by Step
Compare	[product] versus [product]	

Source: MyWorkfromHomeMoney.com

4) **Offer a bonus along with the affiliate product.** This could be a short guide on how to get the most out of it or other special tips. Make sure the bonus material is complementary and allowed under the affiliates terms. You can distribute the bonus material through email automatically when the reader signs up to your landing page or require them to email you their purchase confirmation.

Great types of bonus material that convert to affiliate sales include:

- Add-ons to the product

- Video tutorials on YouTube or your own site

- Quick start guides and How-To

5) Promote your comparison posts and affiliate reviews through social media as you would any other post. Some affiliates will also allow you to **link directly to their site from your social media posts**. These do not generally convert very well and may lead to a few 'unfollows' so I only use them for special offers.

As someone signed up for a company's affiliate program, you will occasionally receive emails about a limited-time or special price offer. Promoting these through social media work best and don't usually peeve readers off.

6) Consider dropping your **affiliate links in your blogroll or a sidebar list** if the affiliate has a blog or other resource for readers. These simple lists don't generally lead to much unless you've got a large traffic base but it's easy to put together and you've already got a blogroll page anyway.

7) **Put affiliate recommendations in your emails and newsletters**. Trust is the biggest hurdle to overcome in affiliate marketing. Readers need to trust you and the recommendation to

actually click through and buy the product. You're already halfway there with your email subscribers who presumably trust you to a point or they wouldn't have signed up for your list.

This can be done through referring subscribers directly to the affiliate through your link or just suggesting your review post and linking back to your blog.

8) **Banner Ads** still can get you some affiliate sales even though it can take over 300 visitors to get just one click...and then 100 clicks to get a sale. Good banner ad positions are up in your website header, to the right of your logo, and in your sidebar. These will show on every page so you'll get lots of impressions and maybe a few clicks. Include text content like your most popular posts and a list of your product reviews in the sidebar as well so it doesn't look like one big commercial.

3 Blogging Affiliate Marketing Rules to Live By

A few pointers beyond what we've already covered. Some are repeats from what I talked about in the affiliate marketing process but are important enough to be added here as well.

- **Remember what your mother said**, "If you don't have anything nice to say..." You need to be honest about an affiliate product but just don't talk about the affiliate if all you have to say is bad. You won't get any sales anyway and I know one blogger that has been sued multiple times because he posted borderline disparaging comments about a few products.

- **Link images with your affiliate link.** Include an image of the product or service next to the content link for your affiliate. Go to Edit on the image details and the Link To drop-down box for Custom URL. This will allow you to paste in your affiliate link so a reader will go to the website when they click on the image.

- **Always make your affiliate links 'NoFollow'.** Google doesn't want affiliate posts to choke its search results so could penalize your blog or individual posts with too many affiliate links. This is easy enough to avoid by marking the link 'NoFollow' which tells search engines to ignore it. You can do this with the check of a box in PrettyLink or through code otherwise by adding rel="nofollow" to the html link.

The affiliate strategy is a crucial income stream for any blog and you won't want to miss out. Find the few products or services that fit best with what you talk about on the blog. Try out a few competing products and promote the ones you like the most.

It's Not Just the Athletes that Can Get Sponsors

Sponsored posts can be one of the biggest money makers for bloggers or they can be a source of constant confusion. I've seen bloggers make thousands a month from the single income source at the same time that other blogs attract no offers.

Getting sponsored posts for your blog is really the first sign that you've made it in blogging. Someone recognizing your blog's value and paying top dollar for advertising.

This isn't the small-scale money you get from pay-per-click ad networks. Sponsored posts earn into the hundreds of dollars for each article.

And I am going to share the exact process you can use to find sponsored post opportunities, how much to charge and how to make more money.

We'll cover sponsored posts from A to Z, detailing everything you need to get started. After a brief definition and how much to charge for sponsored posts, we'll go into how to find opportunities on ad networks and directly with companies.

What are Sponsored Posts?

Sponsored posts are blog articles paid for by a commercial brand or website to advertise their product to your readers. Rather than just a small advertising box as in display advertising, sponsored posts are a much more engaging way to get a product in front of customers.

A sponsored post can be a review of the product or a more indirect approach, talking about a common problem and then how the product makes for a good solution. Sponsored posts include at least one link back to the sponsor's website where the reader can make a purchase or other targeted action.

Sponsored posts are much more effective for advertisers compared to display advertising. Display adds might get a click-through-rate of 0.2% which means just one person clicks on an ad for every 500 people that see it. Sponsored posts can see click through rates as high as 2% to 10% depending on the product's fit with the audience and the quality of the post.

Of course, advertisers pay much more for sponsored posts and it is generally a flat-fee versus the per-click model on display advertising. While an advertiser may offer to pay $1 per click on display advertising, rates for sponsored posts can reach $500 per post or more.

Because advertisers are paying a flat-fee for sponsored posts rather than on a per-click basis or per-sale as we saw in affiliate income, they are only going to be interested in blogs that get a high enough amount of traffic to send them customers. Even on a high click-through-rate of 5% on a sponsored post, only about 50 people will click through the company's link for every 1,000 readers.

Talking about sponsored posts and blog advertising, a lot of bloggers tell me they feel like they are 'selling out' their blog visitors. This is a natural feeling and you shouldn't be ashamed. We all hate commercials and we've all seen spammy websites packed so full of advertising that you can hardly see the content.

You'll get the occasional email from someone complaining about advertising or sponsored posts on your site but the vast majority of your readers will understand that this is a business and you have to make money. Remember two rules when using advertising on your blog:

- Always check out the product and advertiser. For sponsored posts and affiliates, you should try the product out to make sure it's something you feel comfortable recommending. Would you be comfortable recommending it to family and personal friends?

- Build a policy around how much advertising you allow on the site each month and where you allow it. This includes where you place display ads and how many sponsored posts or affiliate reviews you publish in a month.

How Much Money Can You Make with Sponsored Posts?

Like a lot of blogging income streams, how much money you make on sponsored posts will depend on the size of your blog and the topic. I've seen sponsored posts bring in a few hundred all the way up to thousands a month for a blog.

I generally make just under a thousand on the blogs on which I allow sponsored posts, limiting posts to a few per month.

That limit to the number of sponsored posts you publish each month is important. The success of your blog will depend on the community you can build and the trust you have with your community. Post too many sponsored articles and you're more likely to be seen as a commercial than as a friend.

There are bloggers that make their money almost exclusively from sponsored posts but most use a wider strategy. If you're limiting your sponsored posts to a few per month or once per week, you're likely only going to make a few thousand a month even on a very large blog.

Add that to income from display advertising, self-publishing, affiliates and other products though and you've got a great income that isn't dependent on any one source.

How Much Should You Charge for Sponsored Posts?

This is one of the most frequent questions I see among new bloggers. You will start getting spam emails almost immediately after starting your blog from advertisers that want to offer a 'guest' post. Most of these are commercial websites and want to pay all of $25 when you tell them their post falls under your sponsorship policy.

There's an important distinction there. You don't need to charge other bloggers for non-commercial guest posts. Part of your success as a blogger will depend on the community of bloggers with which you interact and exchange guest posts. If a blogger wants to link to one of their affiliate reviews, that's another matter, but generally you won't charge other bloggers just to offer a guest post.

How much to charge commercial (product-targeted) posts is a tough question to answer because the hundreds of low-ball offers drown out legitimate offers at realistic prices.

I've seen all kinds of answers from those roughly based on traffic to one hilariously complex study based on followers, engagement and page views.

I always ask what the advertiser's budget is first before offering a price. This keeps the lines of communication open and avoids missing out on the big dollar sponsors by coming in low.

If you are forced to come up with a number for a sponsored post, there are two ways you can approach it. First is just to price the sponsored post on how much your time is worth. How much money are you making and how much time are you spending each month?

Once you know how much your time is worth…double it and then ask for that amount. It's the first rule in freelancing, always ask for much more than you want and negotiate from there. You'll get a few clients that accept your price outright.

The second way to price sponsored posts is through a common scale based on visitor traffic.

- Start around at least $100 even for a new blog with very little traffic

- $150 - $200 for blogs with 10,000+ visitors

- $200 - $300 for blogs with 50,000+ visitors

- $300 - $500 for blogs with 100,000+ visitors

These rates are for content provided by the sponsor. If they expect you to write the post, add at least $50 or whatever you normally charge to freelance an article.

It will be tempting to drop your price down, especially for new blogs not getting many offers. I would say never drop your price below $75 for a sponsored post. It's not just about the money but the quality of sponsors you'll attract. Pricing sponsored posts for $50 or less is going to fill your site up with all kinds of links to scams and spammy advertisers. It's only going to hurt your brand and credibility over the long-run.

Besides monthly traffic, advertisers like to see social reach as well so work on attracting followers to your social profiles. A massive and engaged social community will more than compensate for lower traffic numbers when it comes to negotiating rates for sponsored posts.

How to Get More Sponsored Posts and Make More Money Blogging

You'll get most of your sponsored posts from three ways; ad networks, unsolicited offers and reaching out to sponsors yourself.

The majority of email offers you'll see will be the spammy $25-type. I reply back with my visitor numbers and social reach, justifying a higher price, but most end up in the trash.

We'll cover pitching sponsored posts in ad networks in the next section. I've had some success with these but have seen the majority of sponsored posts from just reaching out directly to people that have sponsored posts on other sites.

You used to be able to search for 'sponsored post' on another blog and find posts with sponsor links. Google has started cracking down on sponsored posts so most articles don't explicitly say 'sponsored'. You can still find them on other blogs, you just need to look for a few clues.

- Look for posts without a feature image or with a feature image different from the normal format.

- Look for posts with content structured differently than normal. Are there really large content blocks versus smaller paragraphs normally? Is the 'voice' of the writing different?

- Scroll over the links in posts. Links in regular posts will be to authority websites for information or to other blogs. Links to sponsors will usually be to unknown commercial sites.

- Sponsored posts will usually have a link in a short biographical paragraph at the end.

- Check in the blog's 'product reviews' or recommendations' categories.

Paste any links to commercial sites into a spreadsheet then follow the links to find contact information. You'll be using this spreadsheet for years and it will make you A LOT of money so keep it organized.

- One tab (sheet in the workbook) will list all potential sponsors or advertisers along with contact information. Note their product category and when you contacted them last.

- One tab will list all the sponsored posts on your site including URL, price, date of posting and any comments. Have another column list the expiration date on each post, usually one year after publication. This will help with reaching out to people each year for another post.

Your first contact with potential sponsors can be through a simple email. Explain that you saw their post on another blog and thought the product would be a great fit for your audience.

- Explain why your target audience would be a good fit for the product

- Highlight your traffic and social stats

- Highlight click-through-rates on other sponsored posts if available

- Pitch two or three ideas for a sponsored post involving their product

All of this should be in a brief email that takes no more than a minute to scan, use bullet points whenever possible. Don't for get to include your rate for sponsored posts so they don't think you are offering them a free guest post.

You won't get replies from every one of the emails you send but it will produce results, especially for sites over 10,000 visitors. You'll build a huge database of advertisers quickly and can go back to it every year for new posts.

Before you jump into agreeing on a sponsored post, there are a few things besides price that need to be made very clear.

- Links in sponsored posts are generally for one-year. Make sure the sponsor understands this lest they think it's a perpetual link.

- Set guidelines for word length, quality and where the links can point. There should never be any grammatical errors and you should always read through submissions for wording that doesn't make sense.

- Most sponsors will want a dofollow link since this is the one that helps build search power. Google is cracking down on dofollow links out to brands because it recognizes them as paid posts. You can still mark links as dofollow but limit to no more than a few posts each month. The alternative would be to mark a link as nofollow in the html code as in the following example,

<a href="http://www.website.com/"rel="nofollow">Link Text</a>

- Establish who will be writing the post. If you are writing it, will you provide revisions and how many? Will you be providing images? Are there any prohibited words or slogans you're not allowed to mention?

- You must disclose at the top of a post if it contains affiliate links or is a paid post.

I usually require sponsored posts to be paid for within a week of the publication. Send the invoice immediately after publishing and send a reminder after a few days.

Sponsored Post Networks

Rather than reach out directly to potential advertisers for sponsored posts, you can also join a sponsored post network. These are ad networks that connect advertisers and publishers and then take a cut of the payment or a monthly fee. Generally, you will be working with larger brands and you'll be the one writing the posts.

Some sponsored post networks work through ad networks that also offer display advertising options while others only work with sponsored posts.

I've included a short list of some of the most popular sponsored post networks here but there are many more. Those listed here are better for blogs with U.S.-focused audiences and they might not approve you into the network if most of your traffic isn't from North America. Some sponsored post networks also require a certain level of visitor traffic as well.

FederatedMedia bills itself as the world's largest lifestyle network and includes an ad network as well as sponsored post opportunities. The site doesn't list a minimum traffic to be accepted into the network but it is choosy about which blogs get in. The network works with some of the biggest brands like Best Buy, American Express and Old Navy. You can expect rates from a low of $200 and up to $500 for sponsored posts.

It never hurts to apply to ad networks. Even if your blog traffic doesn't yet qualify, it can still put you on their radar for the future. For blogs that do not qualify for Federated Media, the site offers the Lijit advertising network which has no minimum.

TapInfluence is another premium network for sponsored posts. They pay the highest I've seen for posts and directly connect post opportunities with bloggers so you don't have to pitch companies. The site charges brands top dollar for access to publishers so you better believe they place a high standard on who they let into the network.

The network also manages pricing differently than others. You connect your analytics to your account and that determines how much they offer for sponsored posts. You can try to negotiate higher prices if you feel your traffic quality is worth it.

BlogHer is a whole community with an annual conference and educational component. You have to be signed up to the ad network to get sponsored post opportunities but I've heard rates are very good for posts. You can also get sponsorships to promote advertisers through your social profiles if you have a large enough reach.

The network is obviously female-centric. I haven't applied or talked to any guys that are on the network but there are male bloggers on the network. It's a huge community around every blog topic so something to consider even outside of the ad network.

Pitching a sponsored post on one of the networks is a lot like pitching a company directly. You will have already included some of your blog stats in your application to the sponsored post network so advertisers will have access to that information.

For most sponsored posts, you will include a short pitch about a few ideas for blog posts. This is where you emphasize how close a match your audience is with the sponsor and how you want to present the product.

These are mostly marketing people deciding on your pitch for a sponsored post so be descriptive and enthusiastic. Take a day to craft a persuasive pitch on why your blog is a good fit for the brand. You're not just pitching one sponsored post but your relationship with the brand into the future.

Creating a Blog Media Kit for Sponsored Posts and Advertising

While it's not required, accompanying your pitch for a sponsored post will look more professional if you include a media kit. These are one- or two-page documents that detail your blog's value to an advertiser.

Media kits can be made in any format but are usually converted to pdf before sending to a potential advertiser. I've included the media kit for one of my sites here though it's been about a year since I updated it.

There's no required structure for your media kit but there are a few things you want to show advertisers.

- A brief introduction about the blog, common topics and any unique selling points

- A brief intro into yourself and your background

- Social media and email stats

- Traffic stats and demographics of visitors (all available in Google Analytics)

- Keywords and keyword groups for which you rank highly on Google

- Contact information

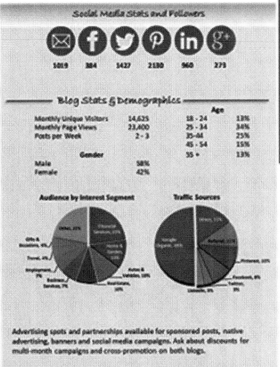

Advertising Rates & Offers

Native Advertising - Review of a product or service in post, > 750 words, keyword optimized and promoted through all social media networks. Limit (2) per month - $200

Sponsored Post - "This post has been sponsored by..." at top of post along with link and choice of 300x250 or 468x60 banner in content. Promoted through all social media networks. Limit (2) per month - $150

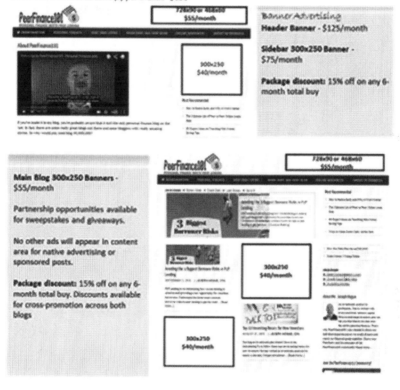

Joseph Hogue, CFA   jhogue@peerfinance101.com   (347) 305 - 0176

You can add your rates to the first page or offer another page just for rates and ad spots. Adding different offers and advertising spots on your blog page or in the sidebar can help negotiate package deals with advertisers.

Sponsored Post Outsourcing and Making Money Freelancing

Sponsored posts are big money for bloggers but another task you have to put on your calendar. Many bloggers put off really organizing their sponsored post outreach and never really see the money they could be making.

This has created a great freelancing opportunity or a way to outsource the work on your own blog.

The freelancer will handle all negotiations and outreach with advertisers. Some freelancers will even publish the sponsored posts to your site if you give them a user account. You redirect any emails for sponsored posts to the freelancer's account and they handle the rest.

I have seen freelancers charge between 25% to 35% of the sponsorship fee. Most just charge this commission rate though some charge a small monthly fee as well. Some have the sponsor make payment to them and then remit to you at the end of the month while some will have you invoice the sponsor and then they will invoice you each month for their cut.

You can see how this kind of a freelancing idea could add up to some serious money. If you manage the sponsorships on just five blogs, finding an average of four sponsored posts each month at about $250 each then you could be making an extra $1,500 a month. Once you've got a list of advertisers that pay for sponsored posts, the whole process is fairly easy to manage for several blogs at once including your own.

5 Mistakes that Will Kill Your Sponsored Post Money

That's what you'll need to get started making money with sponsored posts but there are a few more points that need mentioned. Most of these should be obvious but they're important and I've seen a lot of bloggers commit them and then wonder why they don't make any money.

- **Profanity and poor grammar** – Advertisers may shy away if you use frequent profanity or do not edit your content for grammar. The rule on profanity seems to be becoming more lenient and even 'fashionable' at times but you're still better off avoiding too many expletives.

- **Poorly written or not persuasive** – Not only will a poorly written blog attract fewer advertisers but you just won't see the traffic growth otherwise possible. Check your posts before publishing and then again after their published to make sure they are something people will want to read.

- **Poor blog design or unprofessional** – This is a tough one for those of us 'non-creative' types. A professional, user-friendly blog design affects everything from your reader stats to your rank on Google. Advertisers aren't going to be interested in a site that looks cluttered or unreadable.

- **No contact info or 'hire me' page** – If you are serious about freelancing, put a 'Hire Me' page in the top menu and advertise your services. If you just want to highlight advertising available on the blog, put the page in your footer menu.

- **Not on hosted servers** – You need to have your blog on hosted servers rather than through free hosting on WordPress.com or Blogger. Hosting your site gives you greater control and ownership, something advertisers are going to require you to have.

Getting sponsored posts is one of my top income sources and the process is surprisingly simple once you get organized. Devote a couple of hours each week to finding new sponsored posts clients and keeping your outreach spreadsheet organized. You'll be making money in no time and can even use your list as a freelance tool to make more money.

Self-Publishing:
My Favorite Passive Income Strategy

Most of the millions of bloggers writing hundreds of millions of posts without making a dime have missed one of the best sources of passive income. Self-publishing a book can mean the difference between making real money or quitting your side hustle dreams.

In fact, self-publishing books on Amazon and its related sites has got to be the best way I've found to make money. Self-publishing is a monthly income stream that can be nearly passive once you get started...and it's a natural fit for bloggers.

We'll start off with how to put your book idea together and how to get started before getting to the publishing secrets that will get your book ranked on Amazon.

How much can you make with self-publishing?

All bloggers should be publishing books but even those without an online presence can turn self-publishing into a cash machine to make thousands a month.

I published my first book in April 2015, five months after starting my first two blogs. The book was immediately my top source of income, making nearly $300 a month by the fourth month after publication.

By April 2016, I was making an average of $215 per book each month. I've made an average of $1,500 each month over the last six months. Affiliate and advertising sales on my blogs jumped for a few months but then fell hard in February. Had it not been for self-publishing, which consistently makes more money each month, I may have had to dip into savings to pay the bills.

My Self-Publishing Income

Over $13,000 in less than 18 months through self-publishing with an average of $1,500 each month in the last six months!

$1,603.04
$1,574.60
$1,420.56
$1,102.67
$836.26
$444.89
$308.41
$285.79
$141.86
$15.98

Source: MyWorkfromHomeMoney.com

And I'm not even a stand out in how much money you can make self-publishing. I've talked with several authors that make more than $5,000 a month on 20 or 30 books published on Amazon.

Not only is self-publishing a great source of passive income, something that pays off every month without much work, but it's a natural fit for bloggers. If you've got a website then you already have content you can turn into a book.

Do the math and you'll be an instant convert to self-publishing. You can publish two or three books a year even on a relaxed schedule. You can have between six and nine books published within three years.

If you're making an average of $175 per book each month, that can add up to $1,575 to your monthly income every month!

Keep at it every year and your income will continue to grow.

Traditional Publishing versus Self-Publishing

I get asked by a lot of readers and aspiring authors about the tradeoff between self-publishing and getting a publisher for a book.

While I know authors that have done very well with a traditional publisher, I prefer self-publishing 100-times over!

Let's say you are even able to find someone to publish you book, something that can take years and which frustrates most authors. Publishing your book through a mainstream publisher may still not be all you think it is.

- Publishers will expect you to do most of your own promotional work including traveling for book signing and interviews.
- Traditional publishing can take up to a year or more to work through the editing and printing process. Yours is just one book in their business and it has to sit at the bottom of someone's inbox.
- My experience talking to other authors and a publishing offer I got was that you will get between $0.20 and $0.35 per copy sold.

The upside to traditional publishers is that they take care of all the stuff that you may not understand like editing, cover design and formatting. My opinion is that these benefits aren't worth the costs.

For your first couple of books, you should have no trouble getting friends and family to help with editing. Even if you have to hire someone to edit the book, it can be done inexpensively and quickly.

You can self-publish a book in as little as a couple of months including editing, formatting and a pre-launch period. You may only make a couple of grand on each book so it really isn't worth it if you have to wait on a publisher and can only publish one book a year.

An average e-book is around 180 pages (6x9 format) and between 225 to 250 words per page. Writing three books a year works out to about 10,000 words a month which is very achievable for any blogger.

The best part of self-publishing is the profit authors get compared to traditional publishing. You get 70% of your Amazon Kindle price, so $2.80 on a $3.99 book. CreateSpace takes a bigger cut for paperback publishing but you still get around 35%, or $3.50 on a $9.99 book.

That's about 10-times more than a published author gets for their books…do you think publishers are selling that many more books per month?

How to Turn Your Book Idea into a Money-Making Machine

Too many people get stuck at the starting line with book publishing, stressing out over finding the perfect topic and forming their idea. Even bloggers that write every day become paralyzed by this first step in how to publish a book.

Don't freak out on your book idea!

Mark Twain is quoted as saying, "There is no such thing as a new idea," and remembering that will make coming up with a book idea so much easier.

What do you know? What do you do for a living? Any book that comes from a topic in which you have experience is going to be off to a great start. If you're blogging, then the topic will be the one on which you've written most. If you're not already writing regularly, what do you do for a living or what hobbies interest you most?

Your book doesn't have to be a new topic or about something which has never been explored by another author. Your own experience and perspective will make it unique.

Once you've got a general idea, try doing a search for Amazon books. What are the categories in which the topic shows up? Check out the description and table of contents for each of the first five books to get an idea of what might go into your book.

Go to Amazon's main site, change the drop-down search to 'Books' and search for your topic.

After you've looked through descriptions and the contents of books already on the market, brainstorm what's missing. What can you add that might not be in other books? Check out the reviews for each book to see if readers were looking for something more.

Don't think you haven't got anything to add. If you've got a passion for a topic or have been working in the field for more than a year, you likely know much more than most others.

Now it's time to outline your book, writing out the table of contents and points you want to include in each chapter. Your outline doesn't have to be set in stone. Take a few days to read through anything that's helped you learn about the topic and develop your own guide for the idea.

Of course, the process is going to be a little different publishing your fiction book where you'll need to develop the story and characters. Beyond the actual idea generation and writing, the process for making your fiction book a success is going to be the same as a non-fiction book.

Writing your Book

Stephen King recommends professional authors write 10 pages a day. That might be a little extreme for someone with a day job but you should try writing at least that much a week. I've found that the more detailed you can make your outline, the easier it will be to writing your chapters.

One blogging secret will make self-publishing super easy.

Put together your table of contents for the book. Then plan on writing one chapter a week as a blog post. It breaks writing your book into manageable chunks and you'll have your book finished within a few months.

This makes self-publishing a natural fit for bloggers. You will start ranking on Google for keywords around the book and can link your book's Amazon page into the articles after the book launches. Once you've got all the chapters written, compile them in a single document and add a little extra material so blog readers are getting new value as well.

The most important idea in self-publishing and writing your book is just to keep moving forward on your idea. Don't worry immediately about writing the most amazing content, just get your chapters down on the page. You'll have plenty of time to edit and revise for quality. Too many authors stress out over every sentence and never get beyond chapter one.

Don't Sweat the Little Stuff in Book Publishing

There are a few jobs in book publishing that you'll probably want to outsource or to ask friends and family for help. You could try to do all the editing and formatting yourself but there are a lot of reasons to just have someone else do it.

First, you're just too close to your book to do your own editing and proofreading. As the author, you're more likely to scan over the content rather than give it the detailed eye you need for editing. You'll end up missing grammar mistakes and key developmental issues.

Have one or two friends read through the draft for readability, also called developmental editing. These should be two people with little or no experience in the topic. If they can come away with a good idea of the topic, then you've passed the first editing milestone.

Don't just ask if there are chapters or concepts that could be improved, ask straight questions about the chapters to see how much they learned and to see where the topic is getting lost.

After you've revised the draft according to feedback from your developmental editors, you need to have it proofread for grammar issues. Free is always good so I'd start with asking a few friends to help out. Your book doesn't have to be a grammatical masterpiece so your proofreaders shouldn't worry about finding every little detail. Having more than one proofreader means you should be able to catch 99% of the grammar mistakes.

If you can't find someone to help out on editing, try local reading groups or author exchanges. If none of these are available, then you'll have to outsource the work online. Freelance sites like Upwork and Freelancer will help you find people to do the work but you'll have to be careful to pick quality freelancers.

Editing generally costs between $0.01 to $0.03 per word, with developmental editing a little cheaper. Make sure you phone interview any editors not from English-speaking countries before you hire them. Poor editing can ruin your book and waste all the time you spent writing so it's best to spend a little extra for quality.

After your book is edited for content and grammar, read through it aloud one last time. Don't skimp on this step, it's a great way to catch remaining errors and fix any issues with sentences that are tough to read.

You'll want to have at least three cover ideas designed. You can get these all from the same person or try three different designers. Take these three designs to different Facebook groups and ask people to choose their favorite. This not only helps to pick a great cover that people will like but also helps to build excitement for your book launch. If people think they helped make your book a success by picking an awesome cover, they're more likely to share the launch with their friends.

For book covers, try Fiverr to find a few test designs. Fiverr.com is an online freelancing site where jobs are posted for as little as $5 each. You won't always get the best quality but it's a great way to try out different designers and get a few test designs cheaply.

Finally, you'll need your draft formatted to comply with different requirements on different publishing sites. The version you use to sell books on Amazon Kindle is different than the one you'll need for paperback and pdf publishing.

I generally ask for 5 different formats of the book:

- PDF with the cover image I can use as a pdf ebook
- PDF I can use to upload to CreateSpace and other print-on-demand publishers
- ePub version suitable for publishing to Smashwords, Apple, Kobo and Barnes & Noble
- Mobi version suitable for publishing to Amazon Kindle
- Formatted Word document

As with editing and cover design, you can do all your formatting yourself. Amazon and other book publishing sites provide templates and advice to make it easier. I've always just outsourced it though because I really don't want to take the time to learn the process. It's not lazy but a matter of spending time doing what makes me money, writing. You'll find skilled freelancers to format your book on Upwork for between $100 and $200 for books up to a couple hundred pages long.

Getting your Book in front of Everyone!

One of the details you absolutely must pay attention for your self-published book is converting it into different formats like paperback and audio.

It always amazes me how well paperback and audio books do in sales each month. Paperbacks are more expensive because of printing and shipping. Audio books are priced automatically according to length and usually a little more expensive than the Kindle version.

But not everyone wants to read a book on their computer. A lot of your readers will want the old school paperback version and there is a growing market for audiobooks.

It helps that Amazon owns CreateSpace and Audible, two companies that help you create and distribute paperback and audiobooks. After converting your books, you'll be able to link them to the Kindle version so all three formats are available from one page.

I get about a third of my monthly publishing income from each of the different formats so it is definitely something you can't ignore. You'll be able to convert your book to a print-on-demand paperback easily through CreateSpace and we'll cover some steps for audiobook publishing later on.

How to Publish a Book: The Details that Make Money

You thought just publishing a book was enough to make money? Ha! There are millions of books published on Amazon. It's the details in the self-publishing process that will make you money.

Even if you've already published a book and have your own process, you'll want to read through these next few sections. Your book could be worthy of a Pulitzer but won't make you a dime if you can't get it in front of people.

Building Excitement Before Publishing Your Book

I've had seven books launch to #1 on the best-seller list with four of them regularly ranking within the top five books in multiple categories more than six months after publishing. I couldn't have done it without a pre-launch process and it's one of the critical steps to make money self-publishing.

Up to two months from your book launch, you need to start telling people about the book and building excitement. Ask everyone you know if they would be willing to read the book and leave a review on Amazon during the launch week.

Reviews are hugely important to a book's success. While they don't factor in to ranking within a category, it's social proof you need to make sales. The number of reviews and the stars given on those reviews is one of the first things someone sees when searching Amazon. Having more than ten reviews gives readers the confidence to put down their money and buy the book.

You'll want to post a request for reviews on social networking sites like Facebook and Twitter but don't avoid asking people directly. You'll get ten times the number of reviews by just directly asking your friends and family.

For everyone that offers to review the book, email them a pdf copy for free. Do this at least a month before the book launch to give people time to read the book.

Reviews do not have to be detailed or complicated. Help people understand that all they need to do is click through the link you provide to the review page and jot down a few sentences on why they liked the book. It helps to mention your keywords for the book, more on this later, but really any review is a good review.

When the book is available on Amazon, send the link to everyone that offered to leave a review and instructions on how to click through the page. You might even ask people to buy the book to boost your launch ranking. If you launch at $0.99 then it's not really about the money but about getting those first sales.

If you have a blog, you'll want to create a landing page for your book launch. This is a dedicated page on your website that talks about the book and builds excitement.

Landing pages can be done as a new page but the best ones are done through a plugin like OptimzePress or LeadPages. Using a landing page means there will be less distractions like a sidebar or menus that will take readers away from the page. Create a special offer like a giveaway or discounts to get people to sign up for your email list which you'll use to promote the book launch.

Create a Facebook group for your book launch and change the background images for your social network profiles to feature your book. The Facebook group is a great way to build excitement because you can send out a chapter from the book and have people talk about it and share in the group.

Finally, guest posting on other blogs is a great way to build up to your launch direct people to your landing page. Reach out to bloggers that write about the topic a month or two in advance. It helps to have some kind of a relationship with them before you send your email so follow their blog and leave a few comments on Facebook and on a few blog posts.

Within your email, ask to write a 600+ word post about the topic and to include a link back to your landing page or to the Amazon page for the book. Most bloggers post their guest posting rules so check those out first. Suggest three topics on which you might write a post for the blogger to choose. Don't make the post about your book but about a problem readers might have and how to solve it. Come across as an expert in the subject and people will click through your link to learn more.

How to Create a #1 Best Seller Amazon Book Page

Creating a best-selling Amazon book page is one of the most overlooked steps for new authors. There are millions of books available through Kindle and paperback. Your page needs to stand out if you're going to make any money.

You create your Amazon book page within the Kindle Direct Publishing platform. Click on Create a New Title to get started.

Your book's **title** is one of the most important factors in its success. Just as you did with the cover design, try out a few title ideas on social media to find the one that readers like best.

Every book should have a **subtitle** as well, for readers' and for search benefit. Your subtitle helps readers understand what the book is about and gets them to read a little more beyond your title. Creating your Amazon book page, your title must be exactly as it appears on the cover. This isn't the case with the subtitle and you can add a few of your keywords to give your page a little extra SEO boost.

For example, the subtitle of my Step-by-Step Crowdfunding book is "Everything you Need to Raise Money from the Crowd" but the subtitle I have on my book page is "Everything You Need to Raise Money from the Crowd for Small Business Crowdfunding and Fundraising"

Adding the keywords "small business" and "fundraising" helps the book show up when someone is searching on Amazon and helps me make money.

Your **book description** on Amazon is the most misunderstood tool on the site. Most authors copy down a few paragraphs from their book's introduction and leave it at that, missing out on a huge opportunity.

Your book description is not only important for selling your book to potential readers but a huge factor in getting your book to show up in searches as well.

You are allowed to use up to 4,000 characters (about 600 words) and you should use every one of them. Writing out a description that is persuasive and includes your book's keywords will get more people to buy it and help it show up in search.

Write your book description out as you would an article, with a main headline and headings above sections. You are allowed to use H-tags in your Amazon book description. These are special html instructions that don't show up when people read the description but tell Amazon to highlight and change the size of the sentence. It is also a powerful signal to Amazon and Google on what the book is about.

Use your keywords in the H-tags for your description and your book is more likely to show up when someone is searching for those keywords.

I use the <H2> tag for my main description headline and then <H3> tags for the section headings. Don't think you need to learn html to do a great description. There are websites with tools to write your description and then convert it into the html code to copy into the Amazon description box.

I also use bullet points and call out to specific pages in my book descriptions. For example, every book has a section in the description that says:

In this book, you'll learn:

- How to … (pg. 84)
- Why you need to… (pg. 47)
- …

People are naturally drawn to bullet points as a way to scan content. Highlighting key points and telling readers they will come away with those points by showing them the actual page in the book is a great way to build credibility and excitement.

Finally, use your description to tell people to buy the book and do it several times! Don't just assume that they'll be immediately interested. Ask them to "scroll up and click buy" to keep them from looking around and potentially clicking off the page.

Playing the Category Game

You'll pick two **categories** in which your book will show up on Amazon. These categories follow the BISAC subject codes. The categories you select are extremely important because your book will be competing with others in those categories. If you're not showing up in the top 20 books in a category, you're probably not going to be selling many copies or making much money.

It sucks but there's a game you have to play when choosing categories for your self-published book. Look through a few categories and you'll notice a lot of books that don't seem a perfect fit for the category. Maybe it's something like a financial history book in the online investing category or a book about public speaking in the business management category.

The author has chosen these categories because they are less competitive than the most appropriate category for the book. There are more than 6,200 books available in the Stocks sub-category of Investing but only 717 books in the Analysis & Strategy sub-category. While there might be more people searching for books in the Stocks sub-category, it doesn't mean a thing if your book can't rank highly in those searches.

Placing your book in a less competitive category means you're more likely to get it in front of readers and make more sales.

That said, your category needs to be at least loosely related to your book's topic. It does little good to be one of the first books someone sees when browsing a category if they are in no way interested in your topic.

I follow this process in picking a category for my books:

1. Go to the Amazon main page, change "All Departments" in search to "Books" and click the magnifying glass
2. Scroll down to where you see Books and all the categories on the left-side menu. Each category will have the number of books in parenthesis, i.e. Arts & Photography (1,540,490)
3. Pick a few categories in which your book might fit and click through each individually
4. Each category will be broken into sub-categories and may be broken into categories further within each
5. The fewer books in a sub-category will mean less competition for your book to rank well. I usually try placing my books in sub-categories with less than 2,000 other books.

You'll also need to check the competition within each category by finding what it takes for a book to rank highly. You do this by clicking through the top five or ten books in a category and scrolling down to where you find the Amazon Best Sellers Rank.

The Best Sellers Rank is determined by the quantity of book sales and the amount of sales. A $0.99 book selling a few copies a day will do well but not as well as a $7.99 book selling as many copies. The ranking is of all the books on Amazon and it's important because it gives you an idea of how many books you'll need to sell to have your book do well in a specific category.

The table here shows an approximate from my research for how many daily sales a book needs to rank on the Amazon Best Sellers scale.

Amazon Best Seller Ranking

Rank 200,000 to 100,000	Selling a book a day or every few days
Rank 100,000 to 50,000	Selling 1 - 3 books per day
Rank 50,000 to 10,000	Selling 5 - 10 books per day
Rank 10,000 to 1,500	Selling 10 - 100 books per day
Ranking in the top 100	Selling 1,000+ books per day

Clicking through the top books in a category, if all are ranked better than 50,000 on Amazon, you'll need to sell more than five books a day to compete. That's a pretty tough thing to do as most books will sell less than a book a day.

You can change your categories so it's something you'll want to watch after your book has been published for a month or two. If your book is doing really well, you might consider changing it to a more competitive category where there might be more people searching for books. If it is not doing so well, you might place it in a less competitive category to give it a better chance of showing up in the top 20 books.

Besides the two categories you select on your Amazon book page, there are also 'secret' categories in which your book can be placed. These aren't really secrets in the sense that Amazon doesn't want you to know about them. These categories show up on Amazon but have special requirements so you're not able to put your book directly in them on your Amazon publishing page.

Getting your book placed in one of these categories can be a big win because many are less competitive than the other categories, meaning more sales for your book.

Many of these secret categories have keyword requirements which Amazon makes available in this list. To get your book in these categories, first include the keyword in your Amazon publishers page and within your book description. After your book has been published for at least a month, email Kindle support and ask that your book be added to the category list.

We've talked about **keywords** in other sections but will detail out what they are and how to use them here. On the Kindle Direct Publishing platform page for your book, you're allowed to choose seven keywords or phrases. These are extremely important because it is how people will find your book if they use the Amazon search bar.

Think about the keywords and phrases people that are interested in your book will use. I've included a whole chapter on keyword research in my Google SEO for Bloggers book but we'll go over a few pointers here.

One of the best ways to do this is to start typing a word in the Amazon search bar and see what the site comes up with ideas. These are the most popular keywords for which people are searching so you might want to include them in your list.

Using Google search this way is another good way to find keywords. Start typing a general keyword into Google and it will start showing suggestions. You'll also find suggestions at the bottom of the page with "searches related to [keyword]."

You are more likely to rank better for keyword phrases than single words. Amazon doesn't say how it determines which books are shown when someone searches for a keyword or phrase but besides your book description and keywords selected, your book's rank and sales probably comes into play.

While you might not be able to show up in the first few books for a very broad keyword like "small business" you might be able to for "small business finance". Ranking in the top few books for a keyword, even if it gets fewer searches each month, is more important than ranking at the bottom of the list for a broader term.

Google provides a great keyword tool with the Adwords Keyword Planner. You can use it to get keyword ideas through "search for new keywords" or get the monthly volume of searches with "get search volume…" Adding your keyword ideas into the search volume box will show you how many people search for the keyword each month. This may not show search volume for Amazon but a popular keyword on one is probably popular on the other as well.

Once you've narrowed it down to seven keyword phrases that get a high amount of search, type them into your Kindle Direct Publishing page with a comma separating each.

After your book has been published for a few months, you'll want to start testing different keywords. Record your book sales over the previous month and then try a new set of seven keywords. Do not do any book promoting that you didn't do in the previous month and record your book sales over the next month. Did your book do better with the new set of keywords or about the same? Try this with a few different keyword combinations to see what works best.

Pricing your book is the last thing you'll do in the Amazon page setup. There's a process to pricing just like everything else in how you publish a book and playing with the price can help you make more money over the long-run.

A lot of authors choose to offer their book free for the launch week. The idea is that this gets your book downloaded by thousands of people and the reviews will provide social proof to future buyers. It also used to be a factor in ranking but doesn't help much anymore.

When you offer your book for free, it is placed on the "free" ranking scale on Amazon. Once you raise the price, it goes to the "paid" scale. All your pre-launch efforts and promoting might be able to get your book to the top of the free charts but once it moves to the paid scale, all that effort is wasted.

All those free books that were downloaded don't translate into reviews either. You can expect about one review for every thousand free downloads, maybe less. You need reviews but giving your book away and losing a lot of your launch momentum isn't the way to go.

This is why I've started launching at $0.99 instead of for free. Pricing your book below $2.99 means you'll only get 30% instead of the 70% royalty but it will get you on the paid ranking scale immediately. Paying $0.99 for a book isn't an issue for most people and a lot of people that offered to leave a review will end up buying the book as well if you ask them.

After four or five days at $0.99 for the book, raise the price to $2.99 or higher. This will increase your royalty percentage to 70% and give you a chance to see how well your book does at a little higher price. Since Amazon category rankings change daily, change your book's price mid-day or early afternoon so the price will increase but you'll still be ranked higher in the category.

You can change the pricing as often as you like. I reduce the prices for my books down to $0.99 every few months to promote them and boost rankings. I've found that Amazon Kindle books sell best between $3.99 to $7.99 but some may be able to get a slightly higher price if you've built a following or a name for yourself.

Using Amazon Author Central to Publish a Book

Most of your Amazon page will be set up through the Amazon Kindle Direct Publishing page but a few sections will need to be done on Amazon Author Central. You'll also be able to track customer reviews, book rankings and your overall author rank on the Author Central page.

After you publish a book on Kindle, you'll go to your Amazon Author Central account and add your book to the account by clicking "Add more books."

Click through a book and you'll see a section you can edit for your Amazon page including: Review, Product Description, From the Author, From the Inside Flap, From the Back Cover, and About the Author.

Important, don't touch the Product Description section. The Amazon Author Central platform doesn't allow you to use html code like the H-tags you used on the Amazon Kindle platform. Replacing your book description here will wipe out what you did on the other page.

Once you've got about ten reviews, sort through them for the best four or five and add those to the Reviews section. I also like adding a conversational note in the From the Author section.

Putting something in these sections will show up under the "Customers Who Bought This Item Also Bought" but before your "Product Details" on the Amazon page. It's a good way to squeeze in more reasons for potential readers to buy your book. There are a lot of places a reader can click on your Amazon page that will take them away from your book. Keep them reading good things about the book until they are ready to click buy.

Self-publishing is one of the most passive forms of income I've seen, and I've seen quite a few. From blogging to investing and real estate, publishing a book will provide a stream of monthly income that takes relatively little effort.

Don't Forget about Audiobooks

Like most good ideas…I waited way too long to start selling audiobooks. I didn't think my voice was right for recording and I didn't want to pay high rates to have a voice actor record the books. I don't know anything about audio production and really didn't want to learn.

There are more than three million books available on Amazon Kindle and 31 million paperback titles available on Amazon. Unless you've got a huge blog following or a media empire, it can be nearly impossible to rank in some categories. By comparison, there are only 180,000 titles available on Audible so your chance at ranking well and selling more copies is much higher.

The process for creating and selling audiobooks on Amazon is different from selling traditional books.

1) Read through your book aloud to cut down any clunky sentences and add in any comments that make the reading more conversational. You'll also want to talk through any important tables or graphics.

2) Decide who will narrate your book, where you will record it and who will do the post-production mastering.

3) Plan on about three to four hours of work for every hour of finished audio. Normal out-loud reading speed is about 160 words per minute. The extra two or three hours of work will be spent editing and mastering the audio.

4) I would highly recommend recording in an actual studio. You'd be surprised how much noise there is even in a closed room, from outside noises and even the fan on your computer. Background noise is one of the fastest ways to get your audio files rejected by Audible. Record at a studio and you should be able to get a deal on editing/mastering as well.

5) I found sound engineers with tons of experience on Upwork for about $50 per finished hour of production. Add in another $50 per hour of studio time and other costs and you're at the low end of most estimates I've seen for total costs of between $100 to $200 per book hour.

Non-fiction authors should narrate their own books. You know the material and are passionate about the subject. Don't worry, nobody likes their own voice! Unless you've actually been told its epically annoying then it's probably not that bad.

For fiction novels, it's best to find an actor that can bring out the different roles in a book. Audible makes it easy to find voice actors and studio professionals to record your book but you'll have to share your royalties or pay an upfront fee.

Once you've worked through your book and put together a plan, there are some recording requirements you'll want to follow. Audible is pretty strict about these so make sure you follow them exactly or you might have to re-record your book.

- Record in a WAV format at 44.1 kHz
- Set the recording for a peak of -6 dB and a maximum noise floor of -60 dB
- Set the RMS recording between -23 dB and -18 dB
- Record everything in either all mono or all stereo but not in both

- Read each chapter number and title on each section and leave about two seconds of empty space before you start talking and at the end of the section
- Each audio file must contain only one chapter and be shorter than 120 minutes
- Transfer the WAV files to a MP3 format in 192 kbps or higher and at a constant bit rate

You must include opening credits and closing credits that include the title, author, narrator and copyright information. There are specific things you need to say so I wouldn't stray too far from the script Audible provides.

My opening credits are, "This is the audiobook version of [title]. Written and narrated by Joseph Hogue."

My closing credits are, "This has been the audiobook version of [title]. Written and narrated by Joseph Hogue. Production copyright [year] by Efficient Alpha and Joseph Hogue. The End."

You'll also need a one to five-minute retail sample that will be posted for people to listen before they buy. I usually just use the book's introduction as it's a good mix of sales copy and information about the book.

If your audiobook files are approved for sale on Audible, the book will be automatically priced according to length.

- Books under an hour long are generally $7 or less
- 1 – 3 hours: $7 to $10
- 3 – 5 hours: $10 to $20
- 5 – 10 hours: $15 to $25
- 10 – 20 hours: $20 to $30

It usually takes between four and six days for the book to show up for sell on Amazon and Audible. You'll receive 40% of the sales price for each book unless you split the royalty with a producer. Audible members can buy books with their monthly credit and the payout tends to be about half of what you normally get.

Like I said previously, I get about a third of my self-publishing income from Audible so that's around $60 per book each month. It may not seem like much but it adds up, especially when you have a few books for sale. Audible offers a bonus of $50 when someone gets your book as their first free one on the site.

Self-publishing is one of the best ways to make money blogging. It's a natural fit for bloggers and can be nearly passive after your launch. Not all your books will be New York Time's best sellers but it is a great way to grow your monthly income.

Making WTF Money
with Webinars

I've done webinars before for my crowdfunding consulting and plan on doing more in the future but I have to give most of the credit for this chapter to Steve Chou of My Wife Quit Her Job. Steve sells his ecommerce course through a webinar and is the go-to resource for making huge money with the process.

Using the process Steve shared at a recent conference of financial bloggers, he was able to turn his first webinar into 60 course students at $1,000 each. That's a $60k payout for about 90 minutes of work.

Granted, Steve can spend as much as $10,000 on promoting each webinar but that's still $50,000 in profit. That's one webinar and more money than a lot of people make in a year.

Considering that 83% of bloggers make less than $2,500 a month and only 10% make more than $15,000 per month…Steve's success with his webinars and courses makes him a blogging superstar!

It's not good money…it's WTF money. The kind of money that means the difference between vacationing in Paris, France or Paris, Texas.

The best part is that much of the webinar process to make money is automated. You set up things like your Facebook ads and email series to run automatically and can use most of the same webinar material every time.

Steve now does a webinar each month and makes between $30,000 and $70,000 each time.

Unlike most of the ideas we've covered in the book, webinars don't usually make money on their own. The webinar itself isn't the product but part of your sales funnel to sell the end product.

So we'll start off with how webinars are used to make money and products you can sell before getting to Steve's process for making huge money with webinars.

How are Webinars used to Make Money?

I've seen bloggers try to sell people into their webinar, charging for a virtual ticket, but it usually doesn't go over very well. Most webinars are promoted as free so that's what people have come to expect.

Try to charge for your webinars and you better warm people up with a lot of buildup on your blog or through other promotional material.

You can use webinars as a one-off product, charging up to $100 for an hour-long presentation. The bloggers I know that do this use a shorter, free webinar beforehand to sell into the actual product so the process we'll talk about here is pretty much the same.

For the most part, Webinars are much better suited as part of your sales funnel to drive people to a higher-priced course or consulting product.

The point about 'higher priced' is important. It doesn't make as much sense to spend the time and money involved in our webinar process below to drive people to lower-priced products like ebooks and printables.

I have paid up to $5 per signup for promoting webinars I've done and Steve spends between $2 to $4.50 per signup to his webinars. Steve's experience is that the average attendance rate on signups is 25%, one person attends for every four signups, and the conversion rate from attendance to product signups is between 5% and 16%.

That means you need as many as 80 webinar signups for each product sale (1 divided by 5% divided by 25%) and it could cost upwards of $400 in advertising. You're certainly not going to spend this kind of money if your products are priced at $50 or below but it makes much more sense if you can sell a $1,000 course.

Understand that you can get this per customer cost down to below $100 through perfecting your Facebook ads strategy. Better targeting can get your ad cost down to $3 per signup and around one customer per 30 signups.

People may not need much convincing to buy your $4.99 ebook or printables. You can sell these through landing pages on your blog. Ask someone to come up with a grand for a course and you better be ready to demonstrate some amazing value and take some time to sell them on the product. That's where the webinar comes in.

What to Sell through Your Webinars

So before you go through the trouble of using Steve's kickass webinar strategy, it makes sense to develop a product that will make it worthwhile.

This product better be high-value and be worth the money you are asking people to pay. It should come from your expertise in a very specific area and be backed by your own personal success. Anything less and people are going to have a hard time justifying shelling out $500+ for the product.

What can you sell that is worth a few hundred bucks or more?

The most common high-value products are courses, classes, consulting and membership sites.

- **Courses**: These are usually a set of pre-recorded videos, workbooks and curriculum to teach someone how to do something. Most are supplemented with regular live Q&A sessions.

- **Classes**: The difference between classes and courses is that classes are generally delivered in a live-video format. You schedule the classes and give people a link to the website or software and then give your presentation live before answering questions. Classes use all the material used in courses as well but are a much more interactive format so you can usually charge more.

- **Coaching or consulting**: This is very much like the class but done on a one-on-one format so can be the highest price charged of the three.

- **Membership Sites**: This is a part of your website that is behind password protection, offering members special content and access to you. Membership sites can be a lot more ongoing work than courses or classes because they have no finite schedule. We'll cover details for setting up and making money on a membership site in another chapter.

The idea behind any of these is that you have special experience into something that will make people money or help them be a better person. Search through online course website Udemy and you'll see that the options are pretty much endless.

Whatever you choose to develop as a course or class, you need to develop it around three ideas:

1. It comes from your own personal experience. You need to be able to demonstrate that you have special insight into the topic that is valuable to others.

2. It comes from an impressive personal win. It's one thing to have worked in a topic for 10 years. It's another thing altogether to have turned your experience into a five-figure monthly income. If you haven't been able to be truly successful in the topic, how are you going to teach others to be successful?

3. Finally, you have to be able to teach others to be just as successful. Try your course out on a few test subjects before the launch. These early test cases will not only help you work out kinks in the material but will be great selling points in the webinar.

That said, one of the biggest hurdles for many people is impostor syndrome. It's that nagging feeling you get that says, "Who the hell am I to be charging people $1,000 for a course?" It's something that even the most successful bloggers worry about but you just have to get over it.

You beat impostor syndrome by being good at what you do. Set high goals for your business and work to reach those goals. Over the course of a few years, you'll build the experience to be able to meet all the conditions above. Look back through your own personal wins and you'll find all you need to justify that value to students.

Developing the actual product itself should be fairly easy at this point. You will be putting everything you did to be successful into a teachable format.

It helps to go to Udemy and check out someone else's course to get ideas on delivery and flow. Most of these video courses are more basic than you will want to make yours but they can still help develop ideas.

Some materials to consider for developing your course:

- **Videos** – Even if your class is live, consider putting together some tutorials that people can watch to help explain important topics.

- **Workbooks** – Students want a detailed and guided process to be successful in the topic. Just telling them what to do isn't enough. A workbook can help organize the process and guide them through each step.

- **E-books and curriculum** – There's only so much you can get across in an hour-long class or a few hours of video. Supplement your course with an ebook that really details the process to be successful.

- **FAQ handout or guide** – You want to highlight and address the common sticking points through a special handout. Putting it in an ebook risks getting buried in the material. People love quick-start guides and it goes for common questions as well.

- **Office hours** – Whether your course is recorded or live, it's always good to offer some kind of live interaction where you can answer questions and offer updates to the process.

Teachable and Udemy are both popular platforms for hosting pre-recorded courses. You may not be able to sell a course for as much on Udemy, the maximum you can charge is $200 per course, so that may affect your decision. On the upside, Udemy gets tons of traffic and can bring more students to your course.

Using Webinars to Make Money

That's a pretty big lead-in to get to our webinar process to make money but it's important to lay the groundwork for why people make money with webinars. We'll first cover how to get people to your webinar and then how to convert them to buy your courses or classes.

Advertising your Webinar without Spending all Your Money

Promoting a webinar is always a sticking point for bloggers. It can be scary to spend a few thousand dollars to advertise a webinar before you've made any money on a product. This is really where testing your course and perfecting it with feedback comes in. Put together a great course that stands a good chance of making someone a lot of money and you'll have no problem investing in marketing.

Your webinar marketing starts with the landing page on your website. This is a page dedicated only to getting people to sign up for the course. Check out Steve's landing page below and note some of these important ideas.

- Use magnet words and direct language like, "step-by-step" and "I'm going to show you."

- Landing pages are made on special plugin software, not an ordinary page on your site. This allows you to focus people on a sign-up button instead of all the clickable options in your sidebar.

- Countdown clocks work great for landing pages. You need to build that sense of urgency in your language that drives people to sign-up now.

- Bullet point your biggest selling points so people can scan the page quickly.

- Get testimonials from people that have tested your course to give readers social-proof of its value and highlight recognizable brands you have appeared on.

- Use your picture to show you are a real person and language that establishes a personal connection with readers.

This is just a one-page snapshot of Steve's landing page. It actually goes on for quite a bit more with testimonials, reasons why you should sign up, his own personal success story and more detail on what you learn.

Landing pages aren't just for products you intend on selling through webinars but can be used for any product or even selling affiliates through your blog. Landing pages are great because they give you the chance to really focus a reader's attention on one idea or product.

I use landing pages for my book launches and get a 10% conversion rate. That means one person signs up to the list for every ten that make it to the page. It may not seem like much but it is much better than other signup forms or list-building methods that may only get one in every 20 people to sign up.

Next is actually driving people to your landing page for sign-ups. I've seen a lot of different advertising methods for these including Google Adwords, email marketing and setting up an affiliate program with other websites. The three methods that work the most efficiently seem to be Facebook advertising, guest posts and banners on your own website.

Guest posts are popular because they don't cost any money but can reach large audiences through other blogs. It helps to have a relationship with the other blogger before pitching a guest post on their website, otherwise they may want to charge for the post.

Be sure to offer real value through your guest post topic. Your post should be at least 700 words and really help the reader solve a problem or offer some great advice. This is your first chance to build credibility with the reader and you'll need to offer a great article if you ever want to post as a guest on the site in the future.

It's best if you can get a link to your landing page within the content of the post but at a minimum you should be able to include a short paragraph about your course and a pitch for the webinar at the end of the post.

Banners and links on your own blog are always an easy option in promoting your webinar. Unless you have a very large website audience, this method may not drive a lot of people to your landing page but has its advantage. The method benefits from selling to a 'warm' audience, someone that already knows you.

Have someone on Fiverr develop a 300x250 and 728x990 size banner images for your webinar and put it in your sidebar and the header to your website. Make sure you update all your most popular posts with a brief pitch for the webinar and a link to your landing page.

The most popular way to advertise a webinar has been through Facebook ads. Facebook is much cheaper than advertising on Google and offers some great targeting options to get your pitch in front of the right people.

I use Facebook ads myself for affiliate posts, book launches and sponsored posts. Steve offers a strategy for three Facebook ads targeted to different audiences.

- Advertise your webinar to 'warm' audiences by targeting visitors to your website and fans of your Facebook page. You target website visitors by placing a retargeting pixel (a short piece of code provided by Facebook) on your website. These people know who you are so you don't have to get over that awareness and trust hurdle.

Make sure you use your picture in the image so people recognize you and feel more comfortable clicking through to the landing page. As with all your Facebook advertising, consider making multiple ads with different headlines, images and descriptions to see which one gets the best click-through rate and the lowest ad prices.

- Another group to target your Facebook ads is to look-alike audiences and to interest targeting. A look-alike audience is one built on similarities with people that like your FB page or based on an email list you upload.

You don't need to use an image with your picture in these because targets don't know what you look like anyway. Try out a few different images to see which work best. Steve shares that he pays between $2.50 to $4.50 per lead for these ads compared to less than $2.00 per lead for advertising to 'warm' audiences.

A final option for Facebook advertising your webinar is just to advertise posts to your blog. Getting people to click through and read your blog helps to transition them into a 'warm' audience. You can pitch the webinar within the post or retarget these people through other Facebook ads.

We'll get into more tips on how to promote your webinar in the next two sections but the idea is to make it irresistible. Offer so many freebies and so much value, highlighted on your landing page, that people feel like they are losing money if they don't sign up for the webinar.

Webinar Email Series to Convert

Getting people to sign up for your webinar is one thing, getting them to actually attend and then pay for your product is another hurdle completely. Besides giving a great webinar, which we'll talk about next, your email series is the way you accomplish all of this.

Steve only starts advertising and collecting emails four days before his webinars begin. This helps to build that sense of urgency into the promotion. It also means that people are less likely to forget that they signed up for a webinar.

His goal for these pre-webinar emails, which he sends each day, is to introduce himself and get people excited about the webinar.

Pre-webinar email #1 gives people a link to add the webinar to their calendar through a service on addtocalendar.com. It also highlights the day and time of the webinar.

Pre-webinar email #2 starts a conversation with questions like what doubts they have about the topic and any questions they may have beforehand. It also provides an outline into what you will talk about in the webinar.

Pre-webinar email #3 includes a video introduction of yourself and some testimonials from previous webinar guests. This is crucial to getting people comfortable with you to get them to attend the webinar and before you pitch your course.

It's said that you need six to eight 'touch points' with someone before they will buy something from you. We are flooded with so many commercials every day that we have built a deep skepticism to any product.

It's why email lists are so valuable to bloggers because you can keep bringing people back to your website to build that level of trust. It's also why ad retargeting has become so popular because it targets people that already have seen you through the website.

Pre-webinar email #4 emphasizes the freebies only available to people on the webinar. These can include bonus material, brief consulting calls and even small prizes.

Steve also sends emails out the day of the webinar as reminders. These are sent 12 hours, one hour and ten minutes before the webinar starts. If you're worried about sending too many emails, you might try only sending the 12-hour and the one-hour reminder on the day of the webinar.

Steve gets a lot of course signups immediately after the webinar but to convert the rest, he uses a system of deadlines and emails afterwards. We'll talk about the deadlines in the next section.

Post-webinar email #1 is the replay of the webinar, in case somebody came in late or wants to remind themselves of specific points.

Post-webinar email #2 offers a summary of webinar notes and includes affiliate links to any resources talked about in the presentation. The email also includes a FAQ video of most common questions, an in-depth walk through of the course and some testimonials of people that have taken the course.

Post-webinar email #3 includes a video of a critique on someone's ecommerce site and a worksheet people can use for their own site. These are freebies that Steve offers that offer great value even if someone doesn't buy the course. The email also includes more testimonials from course participants.

Steve ads a reminder in each email about deadlines for freebies and discounts for the course.

Delivering an Awesome Webinar

I've sat through more webinars than I can count. There's no one way to do a webinar, in terms of information offered, and many bloggers have found success with different methods.

Some people will build up their expertise for half an hour, only leaving 15 minutes or so for information. It works for some…personally, I can't stand it.

If I take my time to attend your webinar, I want to learn something I can use without having to buy the full course or product. If I feel like I've just sat through an hour-long sales pitch, I am never going to attend another of your webinars or buy a product.

Steve lives by the same idea when he gives his webinar. He tries to give participants so much value, so many freebies that they can't help but wonder how great the actual course must be. If your full course can be separated into modules, consider using the webinar to deliver the first or second module and hold the rest for the course.

Don't worry about giving away too much information in your webinar. Give people something valuable, something they can really use and they'll trust you. That trust will go a long way in converting people to your course.

I like to use a combination of face-to-face presentation, slideshow and screenshare in my webinars to engage people and keep them interested.

- Face-to-face presentation is simply you sitting in front of the camera talking to the audience. It works well at the beginning to introduce yourself and make a personal connection.

- Slideshows of PowerPoint slides are important for giving information in bullets. Don't be afraid to use lots of slides, even 70+ slides. This keeps people engaged by not spending too long on one slide and boring your audience.

- Screen share is a great way to demonstrate resources and a process, it adds real value in how-to webinars. Be sure to keep a small box of your face in the corner to keep it personal.

Again, this isn't time to be vague and leave out big chunks of information. Give people something they can use and they will trust you as a source.

Don't be afraid to talk about your course. If you spend 30 minutes offering great value, your webinar participants will give you another five or 10 minutes to talk about the full course. In fact, if you've done a good job offering value then they will be excited to hear what they can get with the full course.

People that have stuck around to the end of a webinar are very likely to buy so give them some individual attention with a Q&A session at the end. Make sure you use the first name of anyone that asks a question in your response.

It helps to have an assistant field questions for you during the webinar, copying them down for the Q&A session. Stack the deck with a few planted questions where you can explain why your course is different and how it can help people.

Steve uses a tiered-deadline for his course, yet another way to build sense of urgency in buyers.

- People that sign up before the webinar ends receive free software, a virtual pass to his conference and a discount on the course.

- Signing up by the second day after the webinar gets the discount and virtual pass.

- Signing up on the last day, the third day after the webinar, just gets you the discount to the course.

Steve targets anyone that signed up for the webinar with another set of Facebook ads offering the webinar replay. You can upload your email list of webinar sign-ups into Facebook to target those people and keep them in your sales funnel.

Webinar Fears that Will Defeat You

Webinars work and are a great way to sell your high-value products but there are psychological hurdles you might have to overcome beforehand. These are the little voices in your head that keep you from even starting a webinar.

- **Fear that no one will show up**. This is all part of learning how to market your webinar. Spend some time learning how Facebook ads work and don't be afraid to put some money in marketing. Understand that even pros like Steve pay up to $5 per webinar signup and it takes almost 100 signups to become one customer.

- **Fear that you don't know how to run a webinar**. Don't make your first webinar the one you spent $5,000 advertising! Many platforms like Webinar Ninja and Go-to-Webinar are cost effective and you can give a couple of webinars to test out your skills. Make these a part of a special offer to your email list to test out your course.

- **Fear of the Impostor's Syndrome**. We talked about this one earlier and it's one that strikes even the most experienced business people. Spend a couple of years to become an expert in your field and work on your own personal success. This will give you the credibility you need to sell your webinar and justify your course.

- **Fearing that you don't know how to sell**. Overcoming this fear comes with your expertise in the subject. There is a point where you realize that your course is so valuable that it sells itself and all you have to do is talk about it. Let your past course participants sell it for you by sharing their testimonials and success stories after taking your course.

If you want to make real money blogging, you need to sell high-value courses and products. Few bloggers ever got rich on $3.99 ebooks and printables. We're talking WTF money that turns a profitable five-figure blog into a million-dollar business. If you want to do that, you're going to need to a longer sales process and there are few ways better than the webinar.

Turning a Blog Around
with Printables

Ask anyone with more than one website and they'll tell you, every website makes money differently.

I make just under $5,000 a month across my six blogs but that overall number hides a big difference in income streams on the sites. My personal finance blog jumped to the top of Google for some strong personal loan keywords and the site makes lots of money for affiliate sales each month.

The story for my crowdfunding blog, Crowd101, was very much different. I struggled to make money on affiliates or advertising. There just aren't that many ad buyers in the space. In fact, I almost gave up on the site when it didn't look like it was going to make any money.

Then I published a book based on what I had learned about raising money in the crowd. The book shot up to the top in several Amazon categories and I've made over $5,000 on it so far. My work on the site also landed my biggest freelance project yet, a long-term newsletter deal for $3,500 a month plus commission.

It was another story entirely on a dating & relationships blog I bought last year. The previous owner had struggled to monetize the site and I hadn't done much better. I boosted traffic by 400% over the six months after taking over but blogging income was only up to about $300 each month.

That monthly revenue is just over half of what I paid for the site, not bad but not nearly what I thought the website could make.

I decided to try one more blogging trick, developing a product that has worked on other websites.

The product is called printables and it can be a great way to monetize traffic that isn't making money on other income streams. Printables work amazingly well on craft and home-school blogs but can be used on just about any website to rocket your monthly income.

I added three printables to the site and made over $1,000 on them in the first three months. I'm on my way to making a grand from the site each month.

Even better is that printables are a completely passive income source that you don't need to manage each month.

What are Printables?

Printables started out just as the name implies. Craft blogs were offering a download of printable designs and patterns.

With the massive success on craft and home-schooling blogs, printables have taken off and are inclusive of any kind of digital download. Purists will argue with me here and say there is a difference between printables and digital downloads but the similarities far outnumber the differences and the strategy to make money is the same.

That means you can think of printables as anything shorter than a full-length ebook and delivered in a digital format over the internet.

- Checklists

- Budgeting and other Spreadsheets

- Workbooks

- DIY Designs

- Coloring Books

- Audio or Video Files

We'll get into the creation process below but basically you are just writing something up in a document or in publisher software and then converting it to a pdf file format.

Printables are usually very brief, from just one page and up to 20 or 30 pages. They involve more graphic work compared to ebooks. Whereas ebooks are generally just text, printables offer eye-appeal with more image overlays and graphic formatting.

Printables are detailed and to the point compared to longer content products. Often, printables offer a how-to approach to a very niche topic.

How do Printables Make Money?

Printables are sold directly on your website, you control the pricing and collect all the profit. That's a nice change from selling products on other platforms like through Amazon where you may only get 35% of the sales price.

To make money on printables, you simply create an account with payment software (more on this below) and set up the links on your blog. Once it's set up, a printable is completely passive income. A visitor clicks on the link, pays for the product and is automatically sent a link to the downloadable printable.

Printables are much easier and faster to create than a full-length ebook. They are also very flexible and targeted. Since you can put together a printable quickly, you can design many for very specific topics and place them strategically on your website.

One of the strategies we'll talk about below is creating a printable for a specific post. If one of your popular posts isn't making money like it should, you can quickly create a printable with more detailed information and sell it in the post. That's super-targeting since you know people coming to that post through Google search are going to be looking for exactly that kind of information.

Since printables are generally low-cost products, you don't need the sales funnel you might need to sell higher-price products. You can usually sell printables with a one or two-paragraph lead and some bullet points before offering your buy button or link.

How to Create a Passive Income Stream with Printables

The creation process and pricing for printables is a lot like publishing a book though there are design differences. Like most of the ways to make money blogging, there's no one process you must follow but this one has worked for me.

Creating a Printable that Makes Money

There are two ways I like to get ideas for printables.

The first is just to look at the basic topic for a blog and then narrow it down. Printables need to be very detailed but brief so you'll need a very specific idea or need to satisfy. You're not going to do a printable on 'personal finance' but you might put one together on 'paying off your debt using a specific process'.

This kind of printable is going to make money on your site because it relates to the larger theme and will interest a lot of the people that read your blog.

Another great way to get printable ideas is through your top-performing posts. Some of the most popular posts on my blogs just don't make much money. They get thousands of visitors a month from Google search but there aren't many related affiliates or other things I can promote.

The best way to make money off these articles is to create a printable around the post topic. It needs to be some need or question left unanswered by the post, something else within the topic that people need. Try finding one or two tasks that people need to do within the larger topic and create a printable around how to do those tasks as quickly and easily as possible.

Brief doesn't mean low-quality or of little value. You're saving a ton of time making a printable rather than a full-length book so use some of that extra time to put a lot of detail into the printable. Go through a couple of revisions where you ask a friend to review it and revise with their feedback.

You want your printables to be high quality and visually appealing. Since the price point is low compared to other products, a lot of your readers will buy multiple printables if they are happy with the first.

On design, use lots of white-space in your printables. You want to include call-out boxes, those bordered boxes of text on the side of the page. You also want to border text boxes in things like thought bubbles and speech bubbles.

Your printable shouldn't look like an ordinary book but more like a quality brochure. Add background images behind some of the text and fade the image so the content stands out.

If you're not design-minded, you can find someone on Fiverr to help design your printable. Most Fiverr projects start at $5 but you may have to pay more for the whole project. I suggest hiring a couple different people for smaller design projects to find one you really like then hire them to do your printable design work.

You will also want two banner images to promote your printable. The best banner image sizes are 300x250 pixels and 728x90 which can fit in your blog header, in posts and in the sidebar. Check out banners used by other advertisers for ideas but it should include your cover image and some persuasive text at minimum.

Make more money by making your printable over ten pages. Most printables are shorter than this but create one a little longer and you can upload it as an ebook on Amazon Kindle. You won't want to price it as high as your larger eBooks but you can still make a lot of sales at the $0.99 to $2.99 price point. For the Kindle version, you'll need to format it more like a book without the callout boxes and graphic design.

Make sure you proof read and edit your printables just as you would a longer book. Ask at least one other person to read through the final draft for readability and grammar mistakes. One or two mistakes may not stand out in a 150-page book but they sure will in a 10-page printable.

Converting from a text document to the pdf format is easy. Click on 'File' and then 'Save As' just like you would to save your work. Then use the drop down box to change the format to a pdf. Your document will be saved and you can open it up as a pdf with Adobe Acrobat.

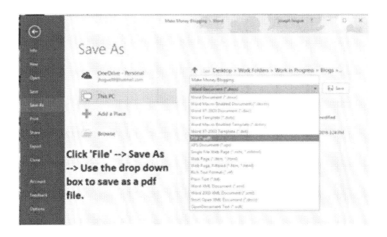

Click 'File' --> Save As --> Use the drop down box to save as a pdf file.

To publish on Kindle, you can use the Word document, pdf, EPUB or MOBI file formats.

I know bloggers that use Microsoft Publisher or other publishing software to create their printables. I've used publisher before to do my own graphic design but I now just put the whole thing together in a word document and have a freelancer from Fiverr do the graphic design. Creating your printable first in a word document gives you the flexibility to turn it into a Kindle book as well as other formats.

How Much to Price a Printable

The biggest mistake in pricing your printable isn't setting it too high but setting the price too low and missing out on making as much money as you could otherwise.

Pricing your printable too low not only means missing out on more money but could mean losing out on sales altogether if people associate the low-price with low-quality.

Check other blogs and books in the topic on Kindle for how other people are pricing their short books. Scrolling down to the specifications section on a the Amazon page will show you an estimate of the page length.

A recent Smashwords survey on ebook prices is also very helpful for printables pricing. The graph shows the number of books sold at each price point compared to a $10 book price. For example, books priced at $0.99 tended to sell 3.9-times as many copies as those priced at ten dollars.

So there's an obvious tradeoff between selling more copies and making money on higher prices. You may sell nearly four-times as many copies at the $0.99 price but you still won't make much money. I've converted the Smashwords survey into a total sales graph to show how much money you might make at different price points for your printable or ebook.

What's the Perfect eBook Price?
Sales for eBooks at Different Prices

Source: MyWorkfromHomeMoney.com, Smashwords (data)

Note that this is total sales on a relative basis. It shows, according to the survey data, that if you sold one copy at $10.50 then you might be able to sell 4.3 copies at the $3 to $3.99 price range and make more money. The sweet spot for printable and ebook pricing seems to be between $2.99 and $6.99 which is exactly what I've found in my experience.

Also note that this doesn't account for fees paid when you sell your printable or Kindle book. You'll generally pay around a 3% processing fee plus a monthly charge to use payment software on your blog and sell your printable. Amazon charges 70% of the sales price for books priced under $2.99 or 30% of the price for books $2.99 or more.

How to Sell your Printables to Make Money

There are two main ways to sell printables on your blog to make money. The first is through your own SSL certificate, a PayPal account and a payment gateway tool.

Before all-in-one shopping cart providers became popular, you would need to do everything yourself. This meant applying for an

SSL certificate to secure the back and forth communication between your blog and a customer. Then you would integrate a payment gateway tool and a payment processor like PayPal onto your blog.

You can still do all this but it's really not worth it and isn't going to save you any money.

The easier solution to make money selling printables directly on your blog is through an all-in-one shopping cart provider like Shopify.

After creating an account on Shopify, you download the Shopify plugin to your blog and connect it with your store name on the account.

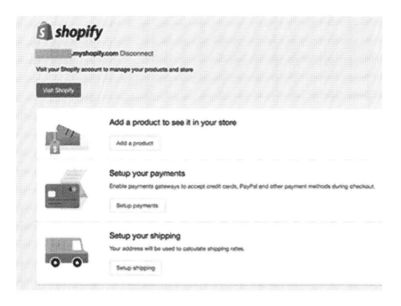

You first add a product with a title, description and price as well as any images. You then link your PayPal account through the email you used to open your Shopify account to receive payments when a product is sold.

Once you've added the Shopify plugin, you will see an 'Add Product' button when you are in your WordPress editor. This will allow you to add your clickable product image into a post or just add a buy button.

Shopify charges $9 a month for the Lite version which is all you need to sell on your own blog. If you haven't got a blog yet, you can open a full store and website through Shopify for $29 a month. Shopify charges $0.30 plus 2.9% of each sale and customers can pay through credit cards or PayPal. You can also accept payments in person through the Shopify app and pay only 2.7% with no transaction fee.

Other digital sales services websites includeSendOwl, e-junkie and Gumroad. They all work identically to Shopify and the setup process is the same.

- Gumroad can accept credit card payments directly, meaning you skip the PayPal processing fee on your sales. Gumroad is also available in some of the countries PayPal is not accepted. There is no monthly fee but you pay 5% of the price plus a $0.25 commission on each sale.

- SendOwl can stamp the customer's name and e-mail on your pdf files whenever they go out, making it less likely anyone will upload your files on the internet for free. The website is best for people that sell in high quantity. There is no per-sale commission but the site charges $6 to $39 per month.

- E-Junkie is one of the most popular shopping cart websites because it charges no transaction fees and is easy to use. You pay depending on the number of products you have available starting from $5 a month for 10 products and storage space of 200 MB. Even with larger ebooks, you shouldn't have a problem with the storage space limit.

Once you've got your store set up to start selling your products and printables, it's time to get them on your blog.

- Update any relevant posts with a paragraph and bullet points about the product along with a link. This is great for printables that are directly related to a specific post or page on your site.

- Create a landing page for each printable. This is a separate page, usually set up on special software like OptimizePress or LeadPages. A landing page is important because it doesn't include your blog sidebar or any of the other options that can distract a visitor. It is just a sales page targeted at one product.

- Include all your products and printables on one products landing page for all the products you sell. This gives you one page to highlight all your products with links or buy buttons to your shopping cart.

You can also sell your printables on Etsy, a marketplace site aimed to crafts and DIY ideas. Selling on your Etsy store costs $0.20 for each four-month listing plus a 3.5% transaction fee on top of PayPal fees. The site doesn't get as much natural traffic as Amazon so you will have to promote your own products.

Some bloggers promote their printables on their blog and then just link to their Etsy store. It works well and is a quick process but I like selling downloads directly from my website. It's just one less click people have to go through to buy the product.

Fiverr isn't just for finding freelancers but can also be used to sell your own products. Since most gigs start at $5 each, it's a perfect price point for selling your printables. Opening an account takes no time at all and you can link it to your PayPal account. Fiverr charges 20% of the selling price which is less than you'll pay on Amazon. The downside is that Fiverr isn't automated like other platforms. You will have to respond to sales and send the files yourself.

Go further with Fiverr and add 'gig extras' which are just product upsells like different services or offers. It's a great way to pull people in for the $5 price and then make a little more money.

Promoting your Printables to Get the Word Out

Paid advertising doesn't normally make much sense for printables. You are probably going to convert less than 2.5% of the visitors to a page into a sale. That means at least 40 visitors for each sale. If you price your printables around $4 each then the max you can pay for advertising would be $0.10 per visitor ($4 divided by 40). That's tough to do when advertising on Facebook, Google or just about any other website.

That's assuming all the visitors to a post even scroll down to see your product. I would say a more realistic average is about 1% of visitors will buy a product which means you need 100 visitors for each sale.

That makes your organic (natural) promotion all the more important.

If you are using a social media management tool like HootSuite, you can schedule to share the posts featuring your products repeatedly. Don't overload your followers with these but I would share a product-related post at least once a day on Twitter and once a week on Facebook.

Don't forget to share on LinkedIn, GooglePlus, StumbleUpon and all the other social networks. Not only might it lead to a sale but it is also going to bring more people to your blog to become email subscribers and regular readers.

You can also use your printables as add-on incentives to sell higher value courses and other products. I usually try to avoid giving away products for free but it's a great strategy to get that sale on a bigger product.

If you are also selling through Amazon or Etsy, reach out to readers for reviews on the sites. You don't need to have bought the product to leave a review on Amazon and it's great for building that social proof that leads to more sales.

The best part about making money with printables is that it is one of the best passive income streams you'll find. Once you have a printable created and linked on your blog, you won't have to do anything to make money. A reader buys the product and the shopping cart system sends it automatically for real passive income. It's a great way to monetize sites that aren't making money with larger products like affiliates or courses.

Call Me Coach:
Six-Figures with Consulting

I've waited to put the coaching and consulting income idea further in the book but it might happen much faster for you.

I've waited to include it because for most people, making money as an online consultant takes more time to set up than some of the other income streams like advertising and affiliate sales. Other people though start their websites for the sole purpose of making money coaching or consulting.

Either way, using your blog to funnel visitors to your business consulting service can be extremely profitable.

Whether you plan on making consulting your first source of online income or working into it more slowly, the process is nearly the same.

How Much Money Can You Make as an Online Consultant?

Payscale lists the median hourly pay for Life Coaches at $30.42 per hour but the range varies from $11.37 to $103.50 per hour and annual salaries go as high as $200,000+ per year. The median pay would work out to just over $60,000 a year if you were working a full-time gig.

That's just one type of coach and doesn't even touch the kind of money some of my financial planning friends make each year.

You can coach or consult on just about everything and we'll get into how to pick your topic later in the chapter. All the hourly rate and annual salary information you're going to see from salary websites won't apply because they are for workers in traditional jobs.

You are going to be your own boss with your own company and that means…

You can make as much money as you want!

We'll cover how much to charge for online coaching in the next section but the idea is going to be to charge premium prices. You are going to be mastering a very focused topic and be transforming people's lives.

You're not just making money for your time, you're earning what it's worth to change someone's life!

How Much Should You Charge for Business Consulting?

This is the first question most people ask before starting an online consulting business. Understanding how much they can charge for coaching gives them some kind of certainty about how much they can make.

But most people immediately doom their coaching business because they try to figure out how much they can charge per hour.

There are two reasons charging by the hour will doom your consulting business to failure.

- Hourly rates sound expensive. Most people aren't going to pay $150 an hour for coaching but tell them how you are going to change their life with a $1,000 package plan and they will click 'buy' so fast it'll make your head spin.People don't pay for an hour of consulting, they pay for you to fix their problems.

- Hourly rates also put you in competition with everyone else charging by the hour. Clients are going to compare your rates to everyone else they find…and will usually end up going with the lowest cost regardless of quality.

Instead of pricing your consulting by the hour, charge according to results. Tell people what problems you will solve and what needs you will help them fulfill. A lot of times, those needs are priceless so you can charge whatever you want.

After working with a few clients, you'll get a better feel for how much time and work it takes to deliver on your promises. You'll be able to adjust your prices higher or lower to find that happy medium between value and making more money.

Three package offers seems to be the sweet spot for selling just about anything online. Each package should offer different results, tools and resources for a little more money. You can target each package at totally different needs or you can make them cumulative where the higher price packages get everything in the lower-price ones and more.

Coaching Plans	Free	$1200 Casual Monthly Rate	$7200 $5040 30% discount Save $2160	$14400 $8640 40% discount Save $5,760	$21600 $10800 50% discount Save $10800
15 min. Phone Call	✓	✓	✓	✓	✓
4 x 60-minute sessions per month		✓	✓	✓	✓
Email support in between sessions			✓	✓	✓
Phone support in between sessions				✓	✓
Partner coached at half price in joint shared session					✓
Duration		1 month	6 months	12 months	18 months

Don't overlook pro-bono and reduced rate coaching for non-profit organizations. You can take the difference between what you charge the organization and your normal rate as a charitable contribution and use it to save money on your taxes.

…OK so you still want to know how much you should be charging per hour for consulting, if nothing else just to figure out how much to charge for the entire consulting process. That's fine. It helps to know your minimum hourly rate to make sure you will make money on your consulting packages.

Follow this process to find your minimum hourly rate for consulting services.

1. How much do you want to make per year?

2. What are the total number of days you can work in a year, i.e. weeks times hours each week? (minus vacation days, holidays, sick days)

   a. Working 52 weeks a year, five days a week is 260 days. Minus 14 vacation days, 9 holidays and 5 sick days would yield 232 working days.

3. How many hours do you work each day?

4. How many working hours can you devote to coaching versus how many are spent on marketing, email, social media, etcetera?

5. **This gives you an estimate for billable hours, i.e. 232 working days times 7 hours per day is 1,624 hours but if only half of the time can be spent coaching then 1,312 billable hours.**

6. If your desired salary included all your expenses then you can just divided that by your billable hours for a minimum

rate. So if you want to make $80,000 a year and can bill for 1,312 hours = $61 per hour is your minimum. Otherwise continue to step 7.

7. Budget out all your expenses including office rent, travel, phone service, subscriptions & memberships, office supplies & equipment, advertising, and services. It helps to look through your business credit card statements over the last year to see everything you've spent money on for the business. Add all your expenses to the amount you want to take home and that is how much money you want to make.

8. Divide how much money you want to make coaching by your billable hours and that is your minimum hourly rate.

What Can You Coach Online?

At this point in the book, you should already know the answer to this one. If there is a website about something…and there's a website for everything, then you can make money coaching on the subject. That's all a website is, a digital consultant where you read about something rather than have someone teach it to you.

There are a few things you can do to make your online consulting business a success.

- Focus on niche within a single idea. It will help you master the topic and stand out among all the other coaches.

  - Master a single need, a single problem that people have within the topic. For example, don't try coaching around the entire pay-per-click (PPC) marketing topic. Instead focus on a specific type of PPC marketing like on Facebook or Google.

That focus is going to help you stand out against all the other consultants that don't specialize.

o   Is there a specific group within the niche above, i.e. Facebook PPC marketing for a specific group of people (bloggers) or an industry (financial services)? Think of this as your 'specialization' within your major. Your extra mastery here will further help you serve specific clients.

- Your coaching should solve a problem. People don't want to 'learn' about your great new technique, they want to solve their problem to which it relates.

You Can Coach Anything

Career Planning	Family Finances	Video Production
Life Planning	Debt Management	Self-Publishing
Investing	Personal Fitness	Fundraising
Blogging	Marketing	Dating & Relationships
Effective Studying	Graphic Design	Starting a Business
Computer Programming	Public Relations	Social Media Marketing
Childbirth	Diet & Nutrition	Home Improvement
Fashion	e-Commerce	Self-confidence

...just about anything!

Don't rule out anything. While researching for this article, I found one guy that was making $10,000+ a month as an online personal trainer. You might not think that kind of face-to-face training would be possible online but you truly can coach anything.

Whatever you decide to coach...your goal should be transformation, not information. Clients can get just about any information free on the internet. They pay you to transform them through your guidance.

Transform your clients and you won't need to advertise for long. You'll start getting more referrals than you can handle.

Local Coaching versus Reaching a Bigger Audience

It may seem a no-brainer, expanding your reach out to as many people as possible. You will probably be doing most of your consulting online so why not offer your services to the world.

There are situations where local targeting is better.

If you are doing professional financial planning or working in other areas like insurance, you may need to work locally because of licensing.

Offering a limited amount of face-to-face consulting for local clients can allow you to boost your consulting package rates as well. It's also going to be easier to rank for your best keywords on your blog if you are including local words like your city or state name. Wrapping your blog content around these local keywords will put you ahead of other consultants that don't have the same focus.

Automating Your Online Consulting Process to Make Money with Less Work

The biggest problem with online coaching and business consulting is that it takes more time than other ways we've covered.

You'll need to constantly be finding new clients, solving their needs and then getting more clients...it's a hamster wheel!

Online coaching isn't a passive income source, but few of the ways to make really big money are truly passive.

The trick to make more money consulting is to automate as much of your process as possible. This means automating both your sales process and the consulting.

Ways to Automate your Consulting Sales Process

- Use the Facebook ads and webinar process we used in the chapter about selling courses online. You'll be able to use the same ads and webinar each month to attract new consulting clients.

- Create a series of emails that go out to all your new subscribers. The first couple of emails should just introduce yourself and build a relationship with the subscriber. The next few emails can further that relationship and build your credibility through personal stories and testimonials. These last few emails also include references to your consulting service and links to the offer page.

A lot of online consultants offer a brief one-on-one session for free to 'qualify' clients and pitch them one of the coaching packages. I'm not a fan of these because it takes so much time to just reach one person. Use the webinar process instead to reach many people at once.

Ways to Automate your Consulting Business

- The idea here is to build out a coaching book to which you can refer and make your job easier. You can create these resources as you go but should put some of them together before you get started consulting.

- o Create all your worksheets and guides you'll use with clients

- o Create videos for every lesson plan or session as a supplement

- o Create a reference resource for all the most common questions and your answers

- o Create a common client persona, a common type of client and their needs, then create a written process that you can follow each time

Starting out, you may need to take on anyone as a client. Eventually, you'll be able to start being more selective and will want to take on fewer client types. This means only taking on clients that fit one of a few 'personas' or needs.

This is going to make it easier to coach each person because they share similar needs and experience. You'll be able to automate more of your sessions and create closer groups, more on this below, which will allow you to work with more clients and make more money!

How to Make Even More Money Coaching with a Mastermind Group

Mastermind groups are more interactive than traditional group coaching but can work with your consulting business as well. Mastermind groups are regular meetings within a topic where everyone adds to the conversation and shared knowledge.

Traditional group consulting means one person does nearly all the talking but has a serious flaw. You always have one or two people in the group that zone out and don't get much from it. It's impossible to transform someone's life if they're just sitting there.

You will still be leading the mastermind group but let people interact, offer their own suggestions and talk about what they learned since the last meeting. It's a great way to keep people involved and take some of the coaching burden off your shoulders.

In fact, some of your mastermind groups may build such a strong connection that members continue to pay you to be a part of the group well after your coaching process has ended.

How to create a mastermind group around your consulting process:

- Break your coaching course into three to five sections, each separated by a milestone people can reach within the section.

- Create a mastermind group for each segment of the course. When someone 'graduates' to the segment milestone, they move on to the next mastermind group. You can also graduate everyone in the group to the next segment, keeping everyone together.

- Segmenting your group coaching like this means someone doesn't have to start at zero in the course if they already have some experience.

- Consider supplementing your coaching groups with a limited one-on-one consulting as well to give each member focused attention.

Making money consulting or as an online coach may be one of the first ways you consider to create income from your blog or it may take a while to build up to it. It's one of the higher-paying online income sources but takes time to build the credibility and experience to be successful. Whichever path you decide to take, don't count out the value of your experience and don't neglect this great way to make money online.

Building Recurring Income with Membership Sites

One of the biggest problems with blogging income is that most of the sources are one-off. You get an affiliate sale or sell an ebook and that's it.

Research shows it can take as many as seven touch points with someone before they buy your product. That means it takes as many as seven times for a reader coming to your blog, reading social media posts, reading your emails or other interactions to trust you enough to buy a product.

The problem in all of this is that it takes so long to convert someone to a customer and so much money…then with one purchase, they're out the door.

It's one of the reasons why it is so expensive to get a customer. You need to be constantly reaching out through advertising or new content to reach new people for a sale.

Don't get me wrong, a lot of bloggers do very well selling these one-time products and affiliates.

And they work their ass off doing it.

Wouldn't it be better if you could keep that customer and turn it into a relationship that makes money every month?

That's exactly the idea of creating a membership site on your blog. Membership sites offer a way to actually grow the relationship with previous customers and turn that relationship into a source of monthly income.

What is a Membership Site?

I'm using the term membership site loosely here to mean any kind of password-protected or members' only content. The most common form of this is pages on your blog that are behind a password protection. Only members may login to access the pages and content.

There are other types of membership sites though. It may not even be a site but a series of emails you send out to members for a course of instruction.

As we'll see in the next sections, membership sites may or may not charge a fee for access. Most charge a monthly fee but others run on hybrid mixes of monthly fees and upsell to members.

How do Membership Sites Make Money?

So there are two ways most bloggers make money on membership sites, either on monthly fees for access to the site or by selling products or services to members.

I like the first method best, charging a monthly fee for membership. It gets you money upfront and you don't have to push people into another sales funnel. It can be a lot of work to set up and maintain a membership site. It kind of sucks when you need to do that plus push further sales to make money.

I also believe that if someone is paying a monthly subscription for access, you need to do everything you can to give them the world. I like being able to focus completely on providing as much value as possible for their monthly fee rather than holding some content back for another product to sell.

The other idea is to charge a little less for membership but then upsell people into products, services and affiliates. While I prefer the other model, this one is a smart way to run a membership site also.

- You get more members on the lower monthly access fee, as long as you're not pricing it so low that people question the value of the site.

- If someone trusts you enough to pay for membership access, they're already primed to take your word on other products.

In reality, the best way to run your membership site is somewhere in between. I tend towards the higher membership fee and then rely less on product or affiliate sales but they do come in occasionally and can make for a great additional income stream.

8 Ways to Create Value for Membership Sites and Make Money

How you provide value to your members is limitless but there are some common ideas that seem to work. These ideas aren't mutually exclusive. You can use one or a combination of several to really give members value for their subscription.

1) **If you are technically-inclined, a software subscription** can make a lot of money and is one of the easiest to manage. Create a WordPress plugin or an application and charge a monthly fee for use.

You'll need to market the software, answer any questions and make sure it stays updated and working but you won't need to constantly create new content or run a membership page.

2) **Drip feed content or courses is a popular membership feature**. This usually comes in the form of a series of emails that go out and teach members how to do something. The 'drip' part

just means that the emails or content go out to members gradually, in a series rather than all at once.

You can deliver all your content through emails or just keep the course material on members-only pages and then link each new part of the course in an email series. I like managing the courses on web pages because it's easier to incorporate video and other materials.

3) **Counseling and consulting services** are another way to offer value to members but these are usually as add-on services rather than something that comes with the subscription. One of the ideas behind a membership site is that it makes money from many customers at once. You can charge more money with one-on-one consulting but it takes much more time.

4) **One way to get around the problem with consulting is to offer Mastermind groups**. These are regular meetings where members of the group share their ideas and help others to solve their problems. Technically, mastermind groups are supposed to be a little more group-led rather than one person leading but they can work here as well.

While you will probably be talking the most and guiding the group, paid mastermind groups can be a great way to build interaction and community among members. It's the sense of community you get from interaction that will keep people in the membership group and keep your income growing.

5) **Monthly services are popular with membership offers**. This may be less like the strict definition of a membership site and more like a business service but it is a great add-on to offer value to your members.

There are a lot of different ways to offer monthly services. It can be a personalized service like offering monthly tech fixes or SEO services to each member. It can also come in the form of a monthly newsletter or content tips.

6) **A community forum is one of the best features you can add to your membership site**. A forum is pages on your membership site that allow members to ask or reply to questions and talk between themselves. You can set member content to post automatically or you can set it so you must approve any questions/replies before they are posted.

There are different levels of control you can take with the forum. The obvious tradeoff is the time it takes to manage and the control you have to weed out spammers or non-relevant content.

The benefit of a forum is that it can grow to sustain itself if you can attract a few active members. A quality forum will be a resource for members. They'll grow to rely on it and the interaction they get and you'll have customers for life.

7) **Some form of monthly live interaction is common on membership sites**. You may be active in the forum or posting content regularly but it's also a great idea to offer a monthly webinar or presentation that details a topic. This can take the form of a group conversation like a Mastermind or a more one-way directional presentation but allowing for Q&A at the end.

8) **Monthly guest speakers are another way to add value for your members**. Besides a way to offer different perspectives and expertise, guest speakers are also a way of getting the word out on your membership site.

Planning your Membership Site

Like a lot of the products or blogging income streams we've talked about, your membership site has to come from a position of expertise and passion for the topic. While some may argue that experience is all that matters, I don't think you can really provide the kind of quality to members if you don't also enjoy talking about the topic.

This doesn't mean you need decades of experience before you can be successful. You'll pick up all the experience and insight you need after a year or two of blogging it. Make sure you check out a few books written by other experts to see if there's anything you've missed but don't wait too long to get your membership site started.

Once you've narrowed it down to a general topic, are there any niches within the topic for which you can create a site. Can you narrow your topic by gender, age or other demographic? The more focused you make the site, the more people will be compelled to join because they'll be able to relate more personally and will feel like it's perfect for their needs.

Next, take a month or two to stalk your competition.

- What are the blogs or other membership sites in the niche? Don't make the mistake of thinking that no competition means a great opportunity. It might mean that there's no money in the idea.

- Don't worry too much about competing with other blogs or membership sites. It's a big internet and providing really great value will bring members.

- Join a membership site or two for a couple of months. What are they doing right and what could be improved?

- How much are other sites charging and are there discounted plans or membership levels? Resist the temptation to set up your membership site as the low-cost competitor. It only hurts everyone by creating a price war and you'll have a tough time producing quality content for the site for the amount of money you make. Instead, focus on how you are going to provide great value and then charge for it.

Top off your topic research with common questions you see on forums, Reddit and Quora. Develop your membership site and content around answering these common questions and your members will see it as a one-stop resource.

Which is the Best Membership Site Plugin?

You add a membership site to your blog through a plugin. The setup to get your membership site started is pretty easy but you'll need to think through some of the different choices for plugins.

There are a couple of free plugins for membership sites but don't get too cheap on this one. Most plugins cost less than $100 as a one-time fee and the extra features can be well worth it to make your membership area all it can be. It's a pain to switch your membership pages to a different plugin after already getting started so take the time to pick the best plugin for your needs.

Some of the most important features to consider for your site include:

- Number of membership levels. While I usually go with just one or two levels, there are reasons to want more membership levels.

- Protecting download content. If your members are able to download content like printables and pdfs, you want to make sure they won't be able to share them with other people.

- Content Access. All membership plugins will let you protect the site-wide content but some will also allow you to sell content on a pay-per-view basis or on other models. It's a nice feature to have if you want to sell individual posts, videos or other content.

- eCommerce features will help you sell other products like pdfs and courses beyond your basic membership access.

- Content drip allows you to plan a series of content to new members directly on the site. This can help keep new members from binge reading all the content and then canceling their subscription quickly.

MemberPress is an easy-to-use and basic membership site plugin that offers most features except ecommerce ability. It's a very popular plugin and the ecommerce option can be handled with a shopify account. The plugin costs $99 for one site or $199 to place on multiple sites.

WooCommerce is one of the most popular ecommerce platforms and the membership plugin looks to be just as popular. The plugin is a little more expensive but offers the ability to create multiple membership levels, both paid and free. The plugin costs $149 for a single site license.

MemberMouse is a monthly subscription plugin which means it costs less to get started but probably more expensive over the long-term. The starter plan costs $19.95 per month while the advanced plugin costs $99 per month though most will be just fine with the starter plan. The upside to the monthly price is that you get better customer service and updates than typically seen with one-time purchase plugins.

My favorite of the membership plugins is the S2 Member plugin. It's one of the few that offer a free version of the plugin. Honestly, many bloggers will do just fine on the free version though the single-site paid version is only $89 and $189 for the multi-site license. It's a one-time fee and the free version can be upgraded to premium if you decide.

S2Member integrates with all the major payment processors including PayPal and Clickbank. It's easy to set up on your blog, discussed below, and the free version includes all the basic features to start a membership site without committing to purchasing the plugin.

How to Set Up a Membership Area on Your Blog

Each of the membership site plugins will need to be configured after installing and it works a little differently on each. I'll walk through the process of getting started with S2 Member but you'll see similarities if you choose one of the other membership options.

First, sign up for S2 Member and select your plan. You can start with the free option. I like the added payment form options with the Pro version and they seem to boost member signups so you might consider the one-time fee for the extra features.

Next, go to 'Plugins' and 'Add New' on your WordPress dashboard to install the S2 Member plugin.

After installing the plugin and entering your password from the S2 Member website, you will need to create two pages to get started.

- **Members** – is the first page your new members will see after they join. I like to use this page to post updates and for a quick list of important pages and news.

- **Subscribe** – This page holds your PayPal buttons and payment levels, or whichever payment processor you use.

The main S2 Member dashboard looks like the screen below. You'll need to change a few of the settings but many of the defaults work well.

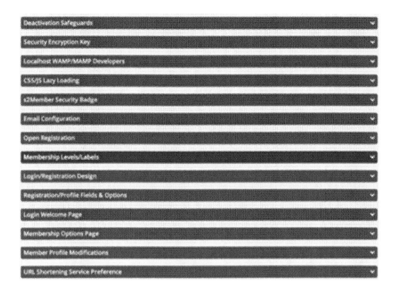

1. Deactivate Safeguards, yes

2. Security Subscription Key, save your unique security key somewhere safe with the rest of your passwords

3. Email Configuration, make sure it shows the email you want to use for the membership site

4. Open registration, this is yes only if you offer a free level of membership

5. Membership Levels, you can rename your levels to something more persuasive

6. Login Design, add a logo and change the fonts/color to match your website brand

7. Registration Options, I usually use yes for all three of these but it's a preference thing

8. Login Welcome Page, set this to the Members page you created so people will see it when they login

9. Membership Options Page, set this to the Subscribe page you created so people can see your membership options and payment buttons

That's it! You now have a membership site on your blog. Now you just need to link up your PayPal account to start receiving payments.

Make sure to update your Member page regularly to show new members how to find their way around and to best content.

How to Get Members for Your Site

Any time you are asking people to pay for a higher-price product or a recurring fee, you'll need to go a little further in convincing them to make the purchase. We saw this in the webinar and courses chapter and it's just as relevant with membership sites.

We'll start with the sales process first and then look at ways to get people into your membership site sales funnel.

Remember, very few sales happen the first time someone sees a brand or a product. Years of watching commercials on TV and people are blind to most forms of advertising. The advertising that isn't subconsciously ignored is mistrusted as a gimmick.

I hate academic theories as much as anyone but the AIDA acronym is extremely useful in making money blogging and something you need to be familiar using in your sales process.

- Awareness – Your potential customers have to know what the product is and who you are first. Just trying to inform them without converting to a sale will go a long way to building a level of trust they need before they'll be comfortable buying.

- Interest – Get the potential customer interested by showing them all the features included on the membership site and what it has done for other members.

- Desire –Create a real desire in the potential customer by showing them how the product serves their needs. Create a personal connection between the customer, yourself and the product.

- Action – At this point, a sale is almost a given if you've taken the time to develop a relationship with the potential customer and walk them through the other stages.

Just sending people to an advertising page rarely works, maybe converting three people out of 100 into paying customers. Using a sales funnel where you start off by building awareness and interest before pushing the sale can result in much higher conversion of up to 20 customers per 100 visitors.

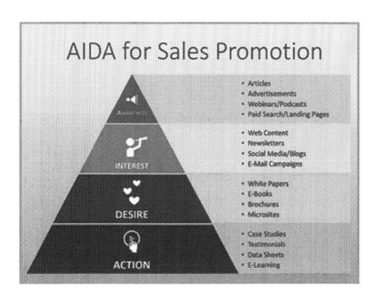

For your membership sales funnel, you might start with a webinar. Promote your webinar through banners or links on your blog that lead people to a landing page sign up.

You can also use an email series as a way to convert visitors into paying members. Set up a landing page to get email subscribers for a special course. This can be a small how-to course within your membership topic or anything that will help your target market solve a problem.

The landing page helps build awareness of your expertise. You then send out an auto responder email series that delivers the course to subscribers. You should offer value in the emails as a standalone but can also pitch the membership site. The idea is that the emails help solve a smaller problem but subscribers will need the full membership access to find everything they need in the topic.

For the actual conversion to membership, I like offering a free two-week trial that automatically converts into a paid membership if not canceled. Free trials are almost expected anymore and you'll have a better opportunity to convert people into long-time members.

There are two ideas in pricing that you might consider:

- Pricing levels and add-ons are always a good idea. Consider discounted levels like a per month membership and a pre-paid six-month membership with one month free. Also, consider adding extra services on higher membership pricing like an hour of consulting every six months.

- Some membership sites offer different levels of access for different prices. This can be a good way of getting people to subscribe at the lower levels and then upselling them into higher levels with more access and higher prices. I'm not a fan of this because it's more work. I also like managing just one membership level where I provide as much value as possible rather than trying to decide how much each payment level gets for its money.

As for getting people into your sales funnel, there are quite a few methods you can try.

- One of the best sources for members is through the email lists from related websites. It's part of the reason I manage six different blogs, building a list of people interested in specific topics but that I can also use to cross-promote different products or services. These lists take time to build but are relatively cheaper than other sources.

- Make sure you check out Steve Chou's Facebook advertising strategy we talked about in the webinar chapter. Too many bloggers are afraid of spending money on advertising but done correctly and it can mean much more income than the cost. It won't take long running your membership site to find how much a new member is worth, basically the average time a member pays dues. This will give you an idea of how much you can spend on advertising to get each new member.

- Banners and links on your blog and in top posts won't send a ton of traffic to your funnel but are a no-cost option for advertising. Generally only about 3% of your visitors will click through a link and then only 5% to 15% of them will sign up on your landing page. That means over 300 visitors for a single signup.

- Affiliate arrangements work well for membership sites. Offer other bloggers or advertisers an affiliate commission for every visitor they send your way that converts to a paying member. Again, you'll need to have an approximate for how much each new member is worth to figure out how much to offer as a commission.

Disadvantages of a Membership Site Income Stream

There is a lot to like about membership sites and they can be a great way to make money blogging but there are also drawbacks.

Membership sites will mean more work and more deadlines. If you promise your members a presentation or fresh content each month, you better deliver. It's not like a blog where you can post whenever you like.

There will be more work interacting with your members as well. Monthly-paying members expect a level of customer service and access to your time. While one-on-one access can be managed by spelling out what members get for their money, you will still need someone to answer questions quickly. Most of the bloggers I know with membership sites have a virtual assistant to help manage questions that come in from members.

This all means that membership sites are much less passive than other sources of blogging income like affiliate marketing. One of the reasons I love self-publishing so much is that book sales are so passive after a successful launch. Membership sites can be made more passive with a forum or with a drip-feed content that goes out to all new members.

The tradeoff in all of this is the amount of money and income consistency for membership sites.

5 Tips to Get Started Making Money on Membership Sites

1) Get started now on your membership site. As with most of the product ideas in the book, procrastination and self-doubt is your biggest hurdle. Read everything you can to build your expertise in a topic and get started.

Try starting your membership site off with a lower, limited-time price. Offer membership to your most committed email subscribers and some other connections that might be a good fit. Let them know you want to use them as guinea pigs so are willing to let them in at a super-discounted price.

Getting started this way, you don't need books' worth of content for your members. Put together a basic course to get people started and then develop the rest as you go.

2) Join another membership site. We covered this in planning but it's an important one that too many bloggers neglect. You'll learn a lot about the management and value provided in membership sites. Remember though that what works for one blogger might not work for you. Be flexible in how you manage your membership site and what you offer members.

3) The best membership sites have engaged and interactive owners. Providing a regular stream of advice is fine but members can get that anywhere...for free. Members join because of your story and your success. Keeping this personal connection is the best way to keep members active. Engage in conversations and be a real resource for members.

4) Group events and challenges are a great way to keep members active and take some work off your plate. These can be monthly or quarterly challenges, where you propose a topic and metrics to reach and then guide the conversation around it. Get people to work in teams outside of the presentations or conversations, helping each other meet the challenge. Small prizes can help to

incentivize people to participate and the interaction will really help build a community of members.

5) Invite influencers or a few people you know will be active to join for free. You might also consider offering discounts to different demographic groups or around holidays and awareness months. For example, promote a big discount for veterans around Veteran's Day.

Setting up and managing a membership site can be a lot of work but it is one of the highest-paying ways to make money blogging. Instead of spending all your time trying to find new customers, membership sites offer the opportunity to spend more time creating value for existing customers and to make more money.

Making Money in Paradise
with Seminars and Workshops

Have you ever looked at the registration costs for seminars, workshops and conferences and thought the organizers must be making a fortune?

Seriously, working as an investment analyst, my boss used to send me to conferences that cost $2,000 just to attend. Even cheaper workshops I've been to started out at $250 and had between 20 and 30 people attending.

It seems like a lot more money than we've seen in other products in the book. It's certainly more than the $0.01 per page view average you get from pay-per-click advertising.

But can you make money with seminars and other events? How hard is it to organize a conference and how much does it cost to run a workshop?

You'll notice that as we've progressed through the nine ways to make money blogging, the payoff has gotten bigger but so has the work involved.

This last method, making money on special events, is the finale of that trend. The Convention Industry Council reports that meetings and conferences generate $28 billion a year and that's not counting smaller workshops or seminars that don't get reported.

To get your chunk of that, you'll need to go farther than you've gone with any of the other income sources.

Tap into it and you can make thousands and it will take you to paradise destinations to host your event.

What Types of Events Make Money?

The types of events you can organize to make money vary on size of audience, number of days and engagement with participants.

At one end, you've got seminars which tend to be a one-day event between 90 minutes to a few hours or a full-day. You don't have to stick with the traditional definition but seminars tend to also be more of a presentation and one-way type of event versus more activities and engagement in a workshop. The presentation format means seminars can be given to huge audiences even into the hundreds of people.

Usually a little longer than seminars, you've got boot camp events which are one- or two-day intensive workshops to teach an audience how to do something. There's really no difference between workshops and 'boot camps'. Calling it a boot camp rather than just a workshop implies that people will get a fast-paced, learning environment and a lot of value for their money. Workshops are usually limited to 25 people or less to make sure everyone gets a chance to participate.

At the extreme, you've got conferences which are multi-day events including multiple workshops and seminars. These include guest speakers and a lot more organization on your part but can bring in more sponsors and a larger audience.

Instead of organizing your own event, you might also consider acting as a freelance speaker or expert for an existing event. There are speaker bureaus that act as agents for speakers or you can reach out individually to event organizers in your niche. The advantage here is obvious with a more certain profit and much less work on your part organizing the event.

How Much Money Can You Make with Workshops and Seminars?

Surprisingly for as much work is involved, event organizers don't make a lot of money. While you might be able to make several grand a month running a membership site, many event organizers struggle to make money especially on their first few events.

The problem is the costs, which get inflated by speaker fees, location costs, catering and travel. We'll cover some of the costs as well as how to save on a few of them. Besides watching costs, the key to making money with workshops and seminars often comes down to being able to sell add-on products.

Costs are going to vary depending on your type of event. You'll have fewer costs with a seminar because people are only going to be there for a few hours. At the extreme, conference costs can start at $50,000 and reach into $100k+.

Seminar and Workshop Costs:

- Location costs will be higher for a seminar with a larger audience compared to a workshop. A small classroom at a hotel will generally start at a few hundred dollars in smaller cities and range up to a thousand. Larger rooms for a seminar audience will range from a thousand or more.

- The location may include use of audio-visual equipment like a projector and screen or you may have to rent it separately.

- Most seminars don't include food though workshops may offer a lunch. Since the audience size at workshops is smaller, you can usually just take care of this the day of the event by calling out for delivery.

- Workbooks and printed material will be one of the larger costs for a workshop. Prices to print workbooks start at around $2.50 for a 40-page soft-cover book in color but you can get volume discounts.

- Larger seminars may book guest speakers though you'll probably want to save money on your first events by speaking yourself. Speaker costs start at paying their expenses, including a one-night stay, but can easily range into the tens of thousands depending on speaker popularity. A relatively new or unknown speaker can usually be brought on for expenses if they're offered the opportunity to upsell one of their products.

- Marketing will likely be your biggest expense for a seminar or workshop. Beyond your email list, you will want to advertise on Facebook and possibly in relevant magazines.

Add it all up and even small workshops generally cost at least $5,000 to organize. You may be able to defer some of these by seeking sponsors or vendors but most of your revenue will come from registrations and add-on sales.

Ticket pricing is lower for seminars but you can host many more people and hopefully sell more products. Seminar tickets generally range from free to $150 per person. You'll only be able to host around 25 people for a workshop so will need to charge $150 and higher to cover costs plus profit unless you can sell a lot of add-ons.

Most of the workshop organizers I know hope to make between $2,000 to $5,000 above costs per workshop. It's not much but can add up if you host one per month and it's a tax-deductible way to travel the country.

Hosting your event at an exotic locale has its advantages but it also comes at a higher cost. I know seminar organizers that count on the attraction for some beach paradise to draw more people but these locations also tend to be more expensive in venue fees.

Compared to conference costs, workshop costs seem like a bargain. The upside to conferences is that you can get a lot more out of sponsors and vendors which may be able to cover the entire cost.

Conference Costs:

- You can't do all the speaking yourself at a conference. At a minimum, you'll need workshop speakers which will cost travel and expenses for each. Most conferences include at least one keynote speaker which will run $5,000 and up.

- Most conferences offer breakfast for each day. Expect catering to cost from $20 per person per meal or more for larger meals.

- You'll also need a staff to organize and manage a conference which will mean hourly wages and travel expenses.

- Location costs jump with a conference since you will need a larger room for the keynote speeches and several smaller rooms for breakout sessions. You will need the larger (ballroom) for vendors and exhibits. Expect even a small conference in a small city to exceed $10,000 for location costs. The website HotelPlanner.com offers an easy-to-use tool to estimate and book conference and workshop locations.

- Most hotels or conference locations will provide audio-visual resources like projectors and microphones...they better for the amount of money you are paying for the venue.

- Most conferences have at least one reception dinner or event and usually a welcome dinner and a farewell dinner. Reserving a restaurant, hors d'oeuvres and drinks will cost at least $2,000 and up.

- Your printing costs for workbooks may not be as high for conferences but other printing costs will far exceed workshop costs. While you can probably design all your workshop materials, you may need to hire it out for a conference.

  o Booklet agendas and schedule

  o Signage for hallways and inside the meeting rooms

  o Vendor and press kits

  o Session handouts

  o Conference brochures, flyers and postcards

- Marketing for a conference is workshop costs times ten…or more. By the time you are ready to organize a conference, your community is likely much larger so you may be able to save on marketing by recruiting people to help spread the word. Still expect this to be your largest expense and easily into tens of thousands of dollars.

Don't expect to be able to organize a conference for less than $50,000 and that's a low estimate. The upside is that you can host hundreds of participants and vendors will pay top dollar to have access to the group for several days.

We'll cover how to get vendors and sponsors later in the chapter. What you charge will vary on the audience you expect, prior event success, popularity of speakers and the audience's industry.

Even smaller conferences should be able to get at least $500 per vendor for small booths and $1,000 for larger booths.

Conference sponsorships are usually sold in levels, i.e. gold, silver and bronze. You will try to sell one or two sponsors to your highest level then four or five to the next level and so on. Sponsorships will include signage around the conference, a page in the agenda booklet and other mentions as well as letting the sponsor introduce themselves ahead of the keynote speech.

Sponsorships for small conferences generally start around $10,000 or more for your highest level and then ranging to a few thousand for the lowest level of sponsorship.

You will generally try to cover your conference costs through vendors and sponsorships with the registrations representing your profit. Making money on seminars and workshops though usually depends on selling add-on products or services.

There are two ways of thinking about this, either charging a very low registration fee and selling more products or charging more on registration and including more in the workshop. I've always preferred to give people as much value as possible, charging a higher registration but including lots of supplementary materials.

Some ideas on additional products you can sell at a seminar or workshop:

- Video courses or course packages including books, workbooks and videos

- Membership to a mastermind group that meets once a week/month for a period after the event

- Private coaching packages or consulting services

- Access to your membership site or forum

- Printed t-shirts, mugs or other memorabilia

How to Set up a Workshop or Seminar

Now that you know how much it costs to organize a workshop or seminar, you have to ask yourself a few questions.

- Is it worth it when you could create an online course and make just as much money?

- Are you organized enough to create an event? There are a lot of moving parts that all have to be managed months in advance.

- Do you enjoy public speaking and can you keep an audience's attention for a few hours?

I'm not trying to talk you out of organizing an event and you can make money with boot camps, seminars and conferences. Even smaller workshops can make $10,000 each and successful conferences can net $50,000+ for organizers but it is a lot of work compared to the relative at-home ease with most of the other ways to make money blogging.

If you still want to organize an event, you'll first want to sit down and define goals. What will participants get out of it? You're asking people to spend at least a few hundred dollars so they better get some great value out of it.

It will help sell tickets and attract sponsors if your event is in a trending theme. Even if you're planning an annual or regular event, try incorporating a trending topic to each event's theme.

1) I know workshop organizers that started planning the location and other details before starting on the event workbook and course materials. You'll have months from booking your location to the event date but I recommend you put your course materials together before starting anything else. What happens if developing your course material takes longer than expected or if you're too busy organizing the event to get it done?

Seminar participants will only need a booklet with promotional ads on your products or sponsors and some content around the theme. Workshops should include a course book, a work book and potentially a digital copy of the presentation and templates.

2) You will need to book your location months in advance before you can start looking for speakers. You might be able to do some of the sponsorship outreach ahead of this but many sponsors will want to know what speakers you have lined up for the event.

There are two ideas here for your seminars and workshops. You can organize multiple destinations and market to a local audience or you can hold one event and market to a nationwide audience.

I haven't seen anything to make me think either strategy is better than the other. Multiple locations make it easier for more people to attend on lower travel costs but are more expensive and time-consuming for you. The market for a single location is much larger but it's harder to get people to attend on the higher travel costs.

Watch out for holidays or other events that might compete for your audience when booking. Late-spring or early-fall seems to be the best time for many seminars and workshops.

3) Will you have speakers at your event? Workshops are usually a one-person operation but seminars can benefit immensely by including multiple speakers. Different speakers and topics are going to attract different people so you expand your audience by bringing on another person or two.

Instead of bringing on a paid-speaker, consider partnering up with a few other people for your seminar. You not only divide the work organizing the event but you'll tap into the other speakers' audiences and attract more people to the event.

As for keynote speakers at conferences…personally, I hate them. I've rarely heard a keynote speech that I liked and these people charge $10k+ for the time. It's a given that a conference will have a keynote but don't be afraid to schedule a relatively unknown speaker if they can actually offer something of value to the audience.

4) Once you have speakers lined up, you can start to seek vendors and sponsors for the event. Workshops won't usually draw a sponsor but you might be able to interest someone if you are using their software or tools. If nothing else, ask participants to sign up using your affiliate code.

You'll get more interest from sponsors and vendors for seminars or conferences. Offer vendors the opportunity to rent booth space outside the room where speeches will be given. Both sponsors and vendors can be offered space in the event booklet as well as signage. Higher-level sponsors will also get introduction privileges before speeches.

Start by collecting materials from all the other conferences and industry publications in your topic. If someone is advertising in an industry magazine or sponsoring another conference, there's a good chance they'll be interested in yours.

If it's your first seminar, you'll have to pitch sponsors on your existing audience and its demographics. Having a few popular speakers on the team can go a long way in convincing sponsors that you'll get a turnout for the event.

Ideally, you'd like to cover event costs with vendor and sponsor fees so put together a detailed estimate of costs before approaching sponsors with prices.

Starting months in advance will give you time to negotiate prices if vendors don't bite at your first offer.

- Start at least $350 for vendor booth space at smaller seminars. Consider how many booths you can fit in public spaces and try cover to at least a third of your costs with vendors.

- Start at least $2,000 for upper-tier sponsors with at least 10 total sponsors across three levels.

5) Put together your event website or landing page. Your landing page for the event should be up at least a few months before the event so you can offer early-bird registration pricing. Consider having at least three pricing levels; early-bird, normal and late-registration. Being able to show how much someone saves by registering early is a great incentive to drive sales.

Don't forget to figure out your refund policy. Can people get a full- or partial-refund if they ask before a certain date? Can they sell their tickets?

You should have a good idea of what it will cost to organize your event to guide your registration pricing but don't forget to budget in something for profit. The worst you can do is under price your event. A lot of hard work goes into workshops and seminars and you deserve to make money for it.

Don't worry so much that the price is too high for participants. Remember, people buy the transformation, not the information. Sell your event on how it will change people's lives. Convince people that you can transform their life and they will enthusiastically spend a few hundred or more on the registration.

6)Once you've got a landing page with payment options, start working on your sales materials. Offline marketing can be a big part of your advertising for local events while nationwide events will usually advertise more through digital resources.

- Brochures and Print advertising for related magazines and local newspapers

- Learn how to write an irresistible press release and develop a press kit

- Consider a sales funnel that starts with Facebook ads and flows through a webinar or recorded videos

- Use retargeting to reach people that have visited your website or specific pages on your blog

- Consider creating an affiliate program and ask other bloggers in the niche to join. Standard payouts for affiliate programs range from 25% to 40% of the registration depending on price.

You need an overwhelming offer to package with your event, anything you can include to add value that isn't reserved for add-on sales. This can include books, post-event mastermind groups, access to a private Facebook community and video courses.

7) Contact printers at least a month in advance to make sure they'll have enough time. You'll need to print out workbooks, agenda or seminar booklets, evaluation forms, signage and any other handouts.

8) Check with the location and catering one week prior to confirm participant count and make sure the venue will be ready.

9) Check all the audio-visual equipment and setup at the location the night before the event or at least a few hours ahead of time.

This list should get you started on organizing a smaller event like a seminar or workshop. There is a lot more that goes into conference organizing so you'll want to have a few successful seminars under your belt before tackling something bigger.

How to Get People to come to your Seminar

We've covered different ways to draw customers in other parts of the book so I'll try not to repeat too much here. You'll find that many of the best ways to get workshop and seminar attendees are the same as those to sell other high-value products like courses.

Your first step will be to brainstorm everywhere your target audience hangs out both digitally and offline. Digital hangouts include websites, social media groups and forums.

If you have an affiliate program for your seminar, reach out to website and forum admins to place banners and text links. You can also offer to write guest posts that link to your landing page. Remember, guest posts should provide quality information and solve a problem by themselves. They shouldn't rely on someone making a purchase to get value from the article.

Don't immediately spam every forum you find. Try answering a few questions and becoming a member of the community for a few weeks before dropping hints that your seminar is coming up.

A location-based seminar opens up a whole new world of offline and targeted-online marketing. With the trend to digital marketing, you can get some great deals on offline marketing through local newspapers and publications.

You can also target locally through Facebook advertising. When you're setting your audience for the post, include people living in and around the city where your seminar will be held.

Note that depending on how much you are charging for your seminar or how much you expect to make from each participant, some advertising may not be profitable. While you may be expecting each workshop attendee to pay the $250 registration and purchase an average of $100 in products, not all that money is profit.

Think of it like this,

- $5,000 total costs for your workshop, including marketing

- You limit it to 25 students and expect $250 in revenue from each ($6,250)

- That leaves just $1,250 for profit and any miscellaneous expenses

You will need to adjust the numbers for your workshop or seminar, playing around with costs and registration prices, but you can see the profit can be extremely thin if you're talking about running a large ad campaign on Facebook and in local print.

Your digital ads will link to your landing page. If you are having trouble converting landing page visitors to attendees, you might try Steve Chou's webinar funnel which works very well to convert people to high-value products. The free webinar draws people in to a relatively low-commitment product before selling them on the workshop.

Of course, you will want to market heavily to your existing email list and anyone that has visited your blog. These people are already familiar with the quality of your information and only need to be sold on the transformation potential of the seminar.

Making your event a partnership with other bloggers can really help spread costs and increase sales through your combined communities.

If you are going to be successful with events, especially larger conferences, you have to tap into the power of communities to bring people in. I attended my first blogger's conference in 2015 solely because of the great community of people I found on the group's Facebook page.

After the event, make sure you keep that sense of community going with a private Facebook group. If your event is annual, it will keep a constant base of attendees coming out. Even if you're organizing one-off seminars or workshops, the group will attract new members to whom you can pitch your event.

There's more risk and a lot more work in these high-value products like workshops, seminars and conferences. There is also the potential to make a lot more money with these events against the money you make on ebooks and PPC advertising. Give your blog time to grow, build a community and you can make money with seminars and workshops.

A One-Year Strategy for New Bloggers

I waited for more than a year to start my blogs. I knew I wanted to own my own web properties, to make money on my own assets and not have to constantly find freelancing clients or work for someone else.

But blogs just don't make much money, not at first anyway.

I had researched blogging and blogging income to know the sad truth about running a website. Most bloggers quit within six months and only about one-in-five make a living doing it.

I was making good money freelancing, earning $50 an hour writing and had plenty of clients…why complicate my life with a blog?

But there was one voice calling out to me and I think you've heard it too.

It's that voice that's saying, until you become an owner, you will always be dependent on someone else for your financial life. You can never truly be financially independent until you own the assets that make money!

For some people, owning investments in stocks is enough. That share ownership of companies helps them grow their nest egg and they can look forward to retirement in 20 or 30 years.

But that wasn't enough for me. I didn't want to wait to be happy in 30 years or to wait for my financial independence. I wanted to control my own financial destiny and I wanted to start NOW!

So I jumped in and created two blogs. Then I started three more…then I bought another site.

I was working harder than I ever did for a 9-to-5 employer but I was in control and for the first time in my life, I really enjoyed what I was doing. Beyond this amazing feeling of satisfaction, the money started coming in faster and faster.

I got serious about making money blogging after about four months building the first two sites. By six months after starting, I was making almost $900 a month blogging. By the time a year rolled by, I was hitting $2,000 a month consistently.

I just had my best month yet, earning just over $5,000 on the blogs and this machine is just getting started.

Am I some kind of blogging superstar or am I even one of the standouts in blogging? Hell No! I am the poster-child for average, the proof that you can be mediocre and still make big money blogging.

But I treated my blogs as a business, putting in the time to learn how to make them profitable. It's one of the biggest factors in my success and what I hope you will get out of this book.

- Treat your blog like a business. Learn the different ways to make money and how to put them all together in a plan.

- Learn how to get Google love by using SEO. I shared my strategic SEO process in a book and how I've doubled blog traffic in a year.

- Understand how long it takes to make money blogging and stick with it!

That last point is probably the most important of all. There are a lot of tricks that will put you ahead of the pack but there is no secret to blogging. You just have to stick with it and know that the money will come.

I've seen a lot of bloggers come and go, just in the two years since starting my own sites. It's why I wanted to start my Work from Home blog and help others bloggers be successful.

How Many Blogging Income Streams do You Need?

We've covered the nine best ways to make money blogging in the book, from immediate PPC income to thousands on courses and workshops.

Will you need every method to make money blogging? Will you even want to try every method?

I know bloggers that make six-figure incomes on just one or two methods. I've tried each but make most of my money from six of the methods. While you certainly don't need to try all nine or have to build your blogging income from more than a few, there is a very important reason why you'll want to make money on at least a few.

What happens when you rely on just one income source and that source goes away?

I know bloggers that relied almost exclusively on traffic from Pinterest to sell their printables. When Pinterest changed their algorithm, the bloggers' traffic plummeted and so did their income.

Other bloggers rely on Google traffic to drive people to their affiliate posts. What happens when your website gets hit with a Google penalty and your search traffic evaporates? It happens to a lot of bloggers.

That's why you want to build your blogging income on at least three or four income sources. Try out as many on the list as possible and see which work best for your blog.

That trial-and-error is important because different blogs make money from different sources. Across my six blogs, I've got one that has made huge money on self-publishing and as a referral to freelancing work. Another blog frustrated me for the longest time until I started selling printables.

Find what works for you, what you enjoy most and what makes the most money on your blog.

Unless you've got a lot of experience in your blog topic, you probably won't be able to jump in to launching high-value courses and events immediately. That's why I ordered the book starting with the easiest, fastest ways to make money and finishing with the more complicated strategies.

One Year into the Make Money Blogging Series

It's easy and costs next to nothing to launch a blog but the amount of time you can spend will depend on other obligations.

The great thing about blogging is that you can work on it in your spare time until it grows large enough to pay the bills. It will take longer to really build your blog on five hours a week but I've seen it done and you can still be making thousands a month within a few years.

First Months of Blogging

Don't worry about making money immediately. Give yourself three months to get comfortable writing, sharing on social media and just growing your blog.

After a few months, start putting together your plan for making money. I'll walk through a few ideas here but feel free to try any of the blogging income methods to see which work best for you. Your experience and goals for your blog are going to be the most important factors in what you do to make money.

3rd and 4th Month of Blogging

Pay-per-Click (PPC) advertising is the simplest and fastest income source to set up and is first on most blogger's list. You can generally make around $0.01 per page view so it's not going to be much but will give you that first confirmation that you can make money blogging.

After a few months of blogging, you'll start to see your blog do better in a few niche topics. These may be more specific than what you had planned on writing about but for some reason, Google has seen your blog as an authority in the topics.

If you enjoy writing about these topics, writing frequently about them will really drive your traffic and open up the potential for more income from affiliate advertising. This is called a 'content strategy' and is a great way of molding your blog around a specific theme.

It's here that you want to open an account on **CJ Affiliate and a few other affiliate networks**. Look for affiliates within the specific topics you write about and apply for their programs. Once approved, you will be able to go back through old blog posts and update by mentioning an affiliate product.

You will also want to start scheduling an affiliate review or two every month. This is where a lot of your affiliate income will come from because these focused posts are easier to rank on Google and you'll get more targeted traffic.

I doubled my income the first month I added affiliates to the blogs and was making over $1,000 a month within four months. It can be a huge source of income and mean the difference between keeping up with your blog or letting it fall behind in disappointment.

5th and 6th Month of Blogging

It takes time to develop your writing style and learn how to write well. Your writing will improve fast and by the fifth or sixth month, you can start thinking about self-publishing and making money off books.

This means doing some strategic planning to make the process easier. We detailed everything in our self-publishing chapter but here's the outline.

- What topics are most popular on the blog? What is something your readers need to know how to do?

- Search Amazon for books on the topic and click through to the table of contents. This will give you ideas for what to write about and the outline for your book. What are other books covering and what could you add that nobody is talking about?

- Put together a list of 15 to 20 chapter ideas and then narrow it down to 10 to 15 critical to understanding the topic.

- Schedule to write at least one chapter each week or two and post on the blog. This will fill your blogging schedule and get you set to publish your book in five or six months.

- Take a few weeks to combine all the chapters, revise and edit before asking a few people to help with editing.

The process also works with printables though these will take less time since they are smaller. You may even want to turn your chapter ideas into printables for sale if they can solve a problem by themselves.

You will be able to publish your book in digital and print format at once. Consider also recording it for an audiobook and uploading to Audible. An average of $200 per month per book is very doable and you can launch a couple of books a year.

10th through 12th Month of Blogging

By the time you approach your one-year blog-a-versary, you should be seeing steady traffic from Google and other sources. With steady traffic and growing social media communities for the blog, you can start reaching out to companies for sponsored posts.

Resist the urge to accept low-ball offers of $25 and $50 for sponsored posts. Those are just spam emails and not worth diluting your blog with a bunch of sponsored articles. Even at this early-stage, you should be able to get $100 for a post from serious sponsors.

Focus on building out these four or five income sources over your first year of blogging and you can easily be making a thousand or more each month. It may not seem like much considering all the work that goes into setting up and running a blog for the first year but you've laid the groundwork for more money from here.

If you already have years of experience in the topic, you might try developing some courses or consulting within this first year but most new bloggers aren't there yet with their experience. You'll learn a lot about the topic, researching and reading to write each blog post, so you'll be more than ready to launch these higher-value products as you work through your second year of blogging.

Six-Figure Blogging Income and Beyond

Once you start developing the higher-value products like courses and membership sites, you can drop other income streams. I've almost completely dropped PPC advertising from my sites and instead use the ad boxes to sell my own ebooks and affiliates.

Again, don't feel compelled to try any income source if it doesn't feel right. The cost of workshops and seminars compared to giving an online course means most bloggers keep their products digital. Live events might work if you are planning to travel anyway and can be a good way to pay to see the nation.

You wouldn't expect to double your monthly income each year at a traditional job but it's possible in blogging. I've grown my blogging income by four-times over the last year and have products coming out that could double it again over the next year.

I personally know more than a dozen bloggers that make over $100,000 a year and quite a few others that I suspect make much more. That's not even considering the fact that any one of these bloggers could get over $1 million if they decided to sell their blog.

Do you need to make \$100,000+ on your blog? Do you want to make that much?

Six-figure blogging isn't just a dream but a goal easily achievable with some of the high-value products like courses and coaching. Spend a few years growing your blog and you'll have people emailing you asking to teach them. You won't have to spend thousands advertising your course because you'll be able to recruit just through blog traffic.

The great thing about blogging is that you are in control. If you get to a point where you blog is making more than enough each month to cover your income and you want to relax…then relax! Do enough work to keep traffic steady and enjoy life.

A Special Request

I hope you've enjoyed **Make Money Blogging** and found the advice to be helpful in learning just how easy it can be to make money online.

I'd like to ask one favor as you finish reading the book. Reader reviews are extremely important to the success of a book on Amazon. Reviews play a big part in determining the rank of a book and how many people see it when searching.

If you found the book to be helpful, would you please leave a review on the Amazon page?

It's really easy to do and does not have to be a long, detailed review.

Please click here to leave a review on Amazon

- Just go to the book's page on Amazon (or through the link above) and click on "customer reviews" or scroll down and click on "Write a customer review"

- Your review can be as short as a sentence or as long as you like. Just try describing what you liked about the book and any particular points from a chapter.

**I always appreciate honest reviews.
Thank you so much!**

Best Blogging Resources

Blogging is a business! If there is one thing you need to get from this book it's that treat your blog as a business and you will make money.

No business is run by just one person and blogging is no different. You'll need to manage your online empire with a range of resources from hosting your site to finding the best ways to put your products together.

I've referred to the resources I use throughout the book but wanted to include a resources page to put them all together in one spot. Some of the resources below require a subscription fee while others are free. Try out some of the free trials to make sure you like the service before putting any money down.

Other Books on Blogging and Passive Income

Making money blogging is making money on the traffic that comes to your site. That's kind of tough if there is no traffic coming to your site (duh!).

Check out Google SEO for Bloggers for my step-by-step process for ranking on the first page of Google.

This isn't a generic SEO book but a guided process for boosting each post you write. Google ranks pages...not websites. Stop wasting your time with generalized SEO strategies and get the one that will get Google Love for each page on your blog.

Get Google SEO for Bloggers on Amazon, Print or Audiobook

See through the BS and scams in passive income strategies to start building a real source of income today in blogging, real estate, stocks and bonds.

NO fluff, NO theories, and NO sugar coating – just the detailed process on how I put together an income from four sources and make money whether I work or not.

Get The Passive Income Myth and start building real passive income

Hosting Providers

The first thing you need to do to set up your blog is to register with a hosting provider. Web hosts will hold your site on their tech hardware and make sure it's accessible to visitors. Most hosting providers charge between $2.99 to $10.99 per month for starter packages but pay attention to special features in each deal.

Blue Host is one of the most basic hosting providers. You won't get as good customer service as some of the others but it's hard to beat Blue Host prices. A good low-cost option to try out blogging without committing too much money.

Host Gator is more expensive but offers a lot of extra features and is still inexpensive on a monthly basis. You'll get better customer service and website performance compared to the cheaper options.

GoDaddy is the most popular hosting provider and a good in-between choice compared to other options. You get all the customer service and features you need at a good starting price.

Plugins and Tools

Plugins and tools will help you run your blog without knowing a bunch of computer programming. They'll also help you manage your blog in the least amount of time possible.

HootSuite is my favorite social media management tool. Instead of spending an hour every day going to the different social media websites and sharing content, you link up all your accounts in Hootsuite and manage them all from one page. Social media traffic and sharing is a big part of blogging so this tool is a must.

Pretty Link makes the URLs to links on your blog…pretty, instead of a jumbled mess that scares off visitors. Pretty Link is a must for tracking clicks from your website to affiliates and products to make sure you are getting credit for your sales.

Fiverr is my go-to resource for outsourcing and small projects. Freelancers post projects they are willing to do, starting at $5 and up. It's a great site for testing out a freelancer's skills before you commit to a larger project. Fiverr is also a good place to offer your own projects for hire.

Ad Inserter is a plugin that allows you to customize a note to be placed on posts, pages or anywhere on your blog. Helpful for disclosures like affiliate advertising and other disclaimers.

Google AdSense plugin makes it easy to place your Adsense boxes on your blog with just a click.

GetResponse will help make email marketing a breeze with its automated process allowing you to send out series of emails to new subscribers.

BoardBooster is a must for managing your Pinterest account. I get thousands of visitors from Pinterest each month and know other bloggers that get tens of thousands from the social media site. BoardBooster makes it easier by letting you set your pins on an automatic loop so you don't have to go to the site every day to pin.

Canva is a design tool to help create cover and image graphics. Easy tool for feature images and product covers.

DepositPhotos is the site I use to find images for my blog. Don't make the mistake of thinking you can just download images for free from Google, it will get you in a lot of trouble and cost a lot of money. DepositPhotos is one of the least expensive image sources and typically runs special deals.

Affiliate Networks

CJ Affiliates is my favorite affiliate network and has a huge database of more than 3,000 advertisers. Quick paying and great publisher support.

FlexOffers was the first affiliate network I was on but takes longer to pay than some others. It's still a good network to be on and you'll find some advertisers that you won't get on other networks.

Amazon Associates is the site's affiliate network platform. Sign up and start linking Amazon products on your blog to receive a commission. Low commission rates but higher conversions than with other networks.

Self-Publishing Resources

Ablurb is a handy tool to create html for your Amazon description page including H-tags and bolded text. This will help get your books ranked and improve the SEO power on Amazon.

Amazon Kindle Publishing is where you'll go to publish your books on Kindle. Good reporting and an easy system to use.

CreateSpace is a print-on-demand service owned by Amazon. Upload your books to sell print versions directly on the Amazon page.

ACX is Audible...also owned by Amazon. It will take a little more work to convert your books to audio versions but it's well worth and your audiobook will be available next to other formats on Amazon.

Product Tools

Whether you need help creating or selling products, these tools will help you find what you need.

Shopify is one of the largest ecommerce platforms and offers several different solutions. I use it to sell printables and ebooks directly from my blogs. You can also set up a Shopify ecommerce store and sell directly from the page.

eReleases is a great press release provider to get the word out on your event or any large product launch.

Udemy is an online video education platform. Use it to launch your own courses or to learn how to do something by taking courses. The site regularly has offers for courses as low as $15 for hours of video learning. As an instructor you get 50% of the payout on courses Udemy sells and 97% of the payout on students you bring to the site.

Membership Sites

Running your own membership site is easy with the right software.

S2Member is the least expensive membership software because it offers a free version, though you will have show advertising. The Pro version is a better choice and only a one-time fee to include all the special features for launching your membership site.

Member Mouse offers better customer service and software updates on a monthly pay plan. It's less expensive to get started but charges every month rather than one-time. Some great additional features for your money.

Made in the USA
Middletown, DE
02 July 2017